825

BOUNDARIES DIMLY PERCEIVED

Notre Dame Studies in
Law and Contemporary Issues

Volume Three

Volume One
Nazis in Skokie:
Freedom, Community, and the First Amendment
Donald Alexander Downs

Volume Two
Public Virtue:
Law and the Social Character of Religion
Christopher F. Mooney, S.J.

The University of Notre Dame Press gratefully acknowledges the generous support of The Honorable James J. Clynes, Jr., of Ithaca, New York, in the publication of titles in this series.

BOUNDARIES DIMLY PERCEIVED

Law, Religion, Education, and the Common Good

Christopher F. Mooney, S.J.

University of Notre Dame Press
Notre Dame, Indiana

© 1990
University of Notre Dame Press
Notre Dame, Indiana 46556
All Rights Reserved

Library of Congress Cataloging-in-Publication Data

Mooney, Christopher F.
    Boundaries dimly perceived : law, religion, education, and the common good / Christopher F. Mooney.
    p.   cm. – (Notre Dame studies in law and contemporary issues ; v. 3)
    Includes bibliographical references.
    ISBN 0-268-00682-2
    1. Law – United States. 2. Religion and law. 3. Freedom of religion – United States. 4. Education, Higher – United States. 5. Pluralism (Social sciences) I. Title. II. Series.
KF380.M66   1990
342.73'0852–dc20
[347.302852]   89-40393

Manufactured in the United States of America

To Mary and John Gallagher
and to Cathy, Karin, and Mary Ellen
blessed relatives and good friends

CONTENTS

	Preface	ix
Part I:	**Finding the Cultural Matrix**	1
	1. American Law in Transition, 3	
	2. Religion at the Fault Line, 11	
	3. Common Good as Meeting Place, 19	
	4. The Burden of Conversation, 27	
Part II:	**The Riddle of the Establishment Clause**	37
	1. The Founders' Disestablishment, 40	
	The Problem of Original Intention, 40	
	Protestant Hegemony in the Nineteenth Century, 50	
	2. Revising the Founders' Legacy, 59	
	Disestablishment Nationalized, 59	
	A Second Disestablishment, 71	
	A Third Disestablishment, 82	
	3. Reconsideration and Compromise, 93	
	Accommodation as Catalyst, 93	
	The Ellipsis of Interpretation, 104	
Part III:	**Education's Prism**	117
	1. Initiation into Citizenship, 120	
	2. Tolerating the Ambiguity of Knowledge, 128	
	3. Elitism and Value Neutrality, 137	
	4. Law, Religion, and Prism Focus, 148	
	Notes	157
	Index	177

PREFACE

"THE FACT IS," SAID Justice William J. Brennan, Jr., in 1963, "that the line which separates the secular from the sectarian in American life is elusive. The difficulty of defining the boundary with precision inheres in a paradox central to our scheme of liberty. While our institutions reflect a firm conviction that we are a religious people, these institutions by solemn constitutional injunction may not officially involve religion in such a way as to prefer, discriminate against, or oppress, a particular sect or religion."[1] Former Chief Justice Warren E. Burger recognized the problem again in 1971: "candor compels the acknowledgement that we can only dimly perceive the boundaries of permissible government activity in this sensitive area of constitutional adjudication."[2]

These two comments reflect the problem as it was originally posed by the Founders: how to construct and maintain a secular federal government in an essentially religious society. Their constitutional answer has proved so elusive over the years precisely because it was premised upon the existence of a certain cultural scene that inevitably changed with the passage of time. For the Constitution was indeed the product of particular historical circumstances and very specific political polemics. While this fact may rule out a timeless meaning discoverable through textual exegesis, it also constitutes an unquestioned strength. "The genius of the Constitution," writes Justice Brennan, "rests not on any static meaning it might have had in a world that is dead and gone, but in the adaptability of its great principles to cope with current problems and current needs."[3]

This adaptability, I shall argue, is a function of those changes in our culture effected by the catalyst of pluralism. While the experience of pluralism has relativized meanings and values, it has not led to either moral or political chaos. This is because the conviction at its base is that membership and participation in society, both civil and religious, is best when it is voluntary. Our pluralism has thus been limited by history, by the meanings and values we have inherited as our tradition, and by that minimum consensus we continue to share as a people regarding what constitutes our common good. Some conservative thinkers are pessimistic about this concept of common good, believing pluralism to imply that the full human good can be lived out only by retreating into a private and exclusivist sphere. But many liberals are also pessimistic whenever "common good" is discussed because they conclude from our pluralism that any communal vision of the good society can only be secured by intolerance for the rights of individuals and their self-determination.[4]

Is the idea of the common good therefore dangerous? This will depend on whether it is conceived to be an absolute already known, waiting to be implemented, or simply what is minimally achievable at any given time in any given society. In the latter case the common good is not something clearly defined, but something to be discovered through communal search. Whether we Americans are able to recognize what it is for ourselves and our nation as a whole will thus hinge upon our ability to carry on reasoned public discourse, and to rely in such discourse on persuasion, not coercion. How pressured are we to discover some basis for social unity that is respectful of freedom? How compelled do we feel as a people to make some sense out of the myriad changes taking place in our culture? How willing are we to use our public institutions of education, religion, politics and press publicly to search for some level of agreement on those basic conditions necessary to remain a community? In order to face these challenges, future citizens will not only have to be educated in all those diverse values and meanings that are part of our inheritance, but they will also have to be taught, in school, home, and church, actively to cherish social equilibrium and to foster social consensus.

The following pages seek to orchestrate these themes of common good, pluralism and cultural change by looking closely at three institutions in our society whose boundaries intersect at many points and frequently overlap. These boundaries, moreover, appear continually to change as soon as one begins to view them through this larger optic. In Part I I examine the current interrelationship between religion and law in American society. Here cultural development has gone in the very opposite direction from that seen by Edward Gibbon to have characterized the ancient world and, by implication, his own world of the Enlightenment. The religions of the Roman Empire, he said, "were all considered by the people, as equally true; by the philosopher, as equally false; and by the magistrate, as equally useful."[5] Such cynicism has never been part of the American scene. In the United States today law and religion have for each other the very highest respect. And the source of this mutual deference is to be found in the wellsprings of our culture, that source of energy impelling us continually to search for the common good.

In Part II I look more closely at the religion clauses of the First Amendment, in particular the enigmatic establishment clause. I try here to italicize the complexity of the process by which we Americans generally, and the Supreme Court in particular, have come today to understand the concept of disestablishment. I argue that the Constitution is to be understood not as a communication from the past but as a symbol of those moral, social, educational, and political aspirations that have developed over time. Its text, so general and so brief, needed two hundred years of experience and interpretation to produce mechanisms of government that would never have been recognized in the summer of 1787: the present practice of judicial review, the role of the president's cabinet, our myriad independent regulatory agencies, to cite only three examples. Any attempt by the Supreme Court to discern and apply the religion clauses must therefore take seriously modern expressions of that popular sovereignty responsible for the Constitution itself and built into its provisions. The sensitive issue, as I try to show, is not the existence of this historical process, which can hardly be questioned, but how the Court functions within the process, that is to say, what counts for the justices in any given case as a constitutional argument.

In Part III my focus is on higher education in America, an institution not commonly associated with either religion or law. I want to relate this institution both to the fact of our cultural pluralism and to the pursuit of our common good. This interrelationship will be shown to be cemented by American society's yearnings for a new kind of hope, a recurrent hunger for the ideal and an eagerness to effect it in the face of negative cultural pressures. Whether these negative pressures come from a faltering economy or the scandal of social injustice, it is obvious that the aim of education is to act as their counterbalance, one avenue of escape offered by society to the next generation of its citizens, one way for them to learn how to live useful lives as socially responsible persons. This aim is indeed the source of education's continuous need of reform and adaptability, processes not unconnected with society's understanding of the role of law and religion. But the boundaries that are here only dimly perceived are, like the three institutions themselves, phenomena of America's future as well as of its present and past. Only by looking at this whole spectrum of time can we hope to achieve those insights that are the marks of the civilized mind.

Parts of this book have already been published and I want to thank the publishers for permission to use copyrighted materials.[6] I am especially indebted to three persons who read the entire manuscript and offered invaluable criticism: Margaret A. Farley, R.S.M., Gilbert L. Stark Professor of Ethics at Yale University, and two of my colleagues in the Department of Religious Studies at Fairfield University, Professors John E. Thiel and Paul F. Lakeland. The Fairfield Jesuit Community and especially its superior, Joseph D. Devlin, S.J., provided a most congenial atmosphere for my sabbatical leave and did much to facilitate the writing of this book. Helen Zeccola carefully proofread the text, which was typed by Edith Meyer, Teresa Delco, and Lee Mihalik with their usual accuracy; to each I express my sincere gratitude. And to Cecilia and Richard Mooney goes my warmest appreciation for their support over many years.

PART I
FINDING THE CULTURAL MATRIX

GEORGE BERNARD SHAW ONCE quipped that England and the United States were two countries separated by one language. We can say with equal truth, I think, that in America law and religion are two institutions separated by one culture. A classic illustration of the point is that in the U.S. Supreme Court, where on occasion these two institutions meet in the greatest solemnity, Justice William O. Douglas, the Court's most uncompromising proponent of church-state separation, could declare:

> We are a religious people whose institutions presuppose a Supreme Being.... When the state encourages religious instruction or cooperates with religious authorities by adjusting the schedule of public events to sectarian needs, it follows the best of our traditions. For it then respects the religious nature of our people and accommodates the public service to their spiritual needs. To hold that it may not would be to find in the Constitution a requirement that the government show a callous indifference to religious groups. That would be preferring those who believe in no religion over those who do believe.[1]

My theme is that American culture affects both the character of our law, the character of our religion, and the mode of interaction between them. I use the term *culture* as H. Richard Niebuhr uses it, following Bronislaw Malinkowski, to mean the artificial social environment imposed on the natural environment, including language, habits, ideas, beliefs, customs, social organization, inherited artifacts, technical processes, and especially values.[2] I use the term *religion* both in its personalized sense of religiousness and in its institutionalized sense of denominations whose teachings and worship foster such religiousness. I use the term *law* to refer to that institution's whole spectrum, from lawyers and courts to legislators and legislation.

The interaction I will be speaking about is immeasurably complicated by the fact that our contemporary culture is generally acknowledged to be in upheaval. For one analyst of the American scene "a recurring image comes to mind, the image of the earth moving deep beneath the surface, and so transforming the landscape that it loses its comfortable familiarity.... The movements may be slight, but the plates are so massive that along their fault lines even slight shifts cause volcanoes and earthquakes on the surface. Increasingly in recent years, our studies of the public show the 'giant plates' of American culture shifting relentlessly beneath us."[3] Law and religion live on the fault lines of this culture: any tremor immediately affects both the legal and the religious landscapes. As a result these landscapes have been expanding, not contracting. In spite of law's own crisis of authority, its power grows steadily; liberal and conservative alike appeal more and more to courts to solve the most complex societal problems. The influence of organized religion is likewise on the increase; one now hears such expressions as "a religion industry," in the same way as one hears of "a health industry."

Deep beneath these surface expansions, however, lies an underlying spiritual ferment, a conflict in our nation's social ethic that constitutes both threat and promise for America's cultural psyche. In the pages that follow I want to focus on this cultural psyche as it has historically institutionalized itself, first in law and secondly in religion. I then want to sketch the context in which these two institutions have interacted in this country, and to indicate why current developments in each have set the stage for a mutual search to find the common good. Finally I want to speak of religion's burden in this search not to use law badly, either by posing questions that are narrowly sectarian or by insisting upon discussions that are neither provisional nor problematic.

1. American Law in Transition

To appreciate how American culture has shaped American law, we must situate this culture in relation to a larger social experience of the West usually referred to as "secularization." This process is frequently described negatively, as the removal of all sectors of the human enterprise from the domination and control of religious institutions. But I find it far more satisfying to view the process positively, as a permanent change in the human psyche that has gradually come to birth since the fifteenth century as a result of three extraordinary movements of social change. There was first the transition from agriculture to industry, with its huge expansion of commercial resources and its broad distribution of wealth outside the hereditary privileged classes. Masses of people gradually came to a realization, quite new in human history, that they could change the way they lived. It was from this prospect of continuing growth in economic output that a belief in "progress" was born. "The idea that people, even regular people, have a right to expect happiness *in this world* is a key part of the concept of secularization."[4]

The second movement took place in the world of science. Completely natural explanations were provided for physical and chemical phenomena as well as for human biology, all of which were previously believed to be totally mysterious and unknowable. Modern science taught us that we can understand a great deal of the world and that in many cases we can change the environment in which we live in ways never before thought possible. This intellectual revolution, coupled with the economic revolution, led to the third movement, a revolution in the way societies governed themselves. For the rule of an aristocratic elite makes sense only in societies where ignorance and scarcity are widespread. When the West grew affluent, however, various forms of participatory democracy spread rapidly, and in such an atmosphere the areas of science, technology, education, and health care increasingly produced their beneficial effects. It became evident that the visible world could be controlled through human reason, hypothesis, and experimentation. Nature and history were therefore no longer seen to be sacred, nor in themselves immediately dependent on any religion.

This gradual recognition that even the most accepted presuppositions of society could be renegotiated, altered, and perhaps even superseded in favor of conscious human purposes had a dramatic effect in the area of law. Positively, it freed law from theological doctrine and direct ecclesiastical control and enabled it to undergo a new and brilliant development. "The key to renewal of law in the West from the sixteenth century on," writes Harold Berman,

> was the Protestant concept of the power of the individual, by God's grace, to change nature and to create new social relations through the exercise of his will.... Nature became property. Economic relations became contract. Conscience became will and intent. The last testament, which in the earlier Catholic tradition had been the means of saving souls by charitable gifts, became a means of controlling social and economic relations.... The property and contract rights so created were held to be sacred and inviolable, so long as they did not contravene conscience. Conscience gave them their sanctity. And so the secularization of the state... was accompanied by a spiritualization and even a sanctification of property and contract.[5]

But there was also a negative effect of secularization on law. With the explicit denial that it was the church's task to be guardian of human law, there developed a corresponding skepticism that human law ought ever to have been conceived as a reflection of some divine law. The net result was a legal positivism, law understood simply as a means of manifesting and securing obedience to the policies of a particular sovereign power, whether individual or community. With the decline of a single religious source for moral consensus, however, there inevitably increased a demand for the state to regulate moral behavior. The less religion was able to discipline, the more the state was expected to. Right and wrong became what the law said was right and wrong. Because law was understood to be whatever official commands existed at the time, morality came to be seen largely or even exclusively as a matter of rules drawn up into some code. This naturally led to an inflation of all government enterprises. Rendered fragile by the absence of any transcendent justification, political power tended to find its justification in law. This is the point of a remark by Hannah Arendt that secularization is usually accompanied by a rise in absolutism.

All these extraordinary movements of social change were already in place in the West when the United States was born. The Founders saw the nation they created as one in which the separate spheres of politics, science, and commerce had full autonomy and were ruled by their own norms. From the beginning ours was an inherently pluralistic society, with not a trace of nostalgia for a bygone time when a single set of beliefs and ideals unified the whole. In this sense the United States was the first thoroughly modern nation. While there have always been small pockets of Americans who reject modernity, the vast majority have been committed to the idea of progress and the right to pursue earthly happiness and quite content with the naturalism that underlies modern science.[6] Indeed, the democratic process created by the Constitution aimed precisely at giving form, limits, and protection to the rights of citizens and at guaranteeing for them that equality before the law that had become the hallmark and discovery of the age. Inevitably this secularization of society was to influence the development of our legal culture.

This positivistic character of law in the West, which followed from its removal from ecclesiastical control, was from the beginning part of the living worldview of average American lawyers, trained as they were in the tradition of English common law. John Austin, who formulated a theory of positivism in the early 1800s, saw law as a brute social fact based on power, which in turn could be exercised for good or ill. For him laws were coercive commands, whether they be wise or foolish, just or unjust. Hence law did not necessarily serve the common good, nor was it always designed to do so. Oliver Wendell Holmes, Jr., who inherited Austin's jurisprudence here in the United States, defined law as "prophesies of what the courts will do in fact, and nothing more pretentious." Law, he said, "is a neutral object to be used where it might benefit, to be avoided where it might hurt, and to be put into the balance of calculations as one sets out one's policies for the future."[7] For the legal positivists of the last century law was thus law as it is, not law as it ought to be: it represented simply what a society was like at any particular time in its history. It was, as legal historians like to say, "a dependent variable," the product of changing social forces.[8]

The positivists shaped American legal education to correspond with their understanding of law. I have dealt at some length elsewhere with the wider implications of positivism as it has impinged upon legal education.[9] What I wish to emphasize here is that the result was to produce lawyers who by and large deeply distrusted generalizations and had little or no concern for the larger social issues involved in reaching legal decisions. Legal realists, on the other hand, who became the twentieth-century heirs of the positivists, readily acknowledged that law can never be isolated from economic, political, and cultural developments, but they could see no place in legal education for any critical judgment on the social values responsible for such developments, for such values were by definition unanalyzable, nothing more than inscrutable expressions of personal preference.

The task of the lawyer was thus to focus exclusively on the data of a particular case and to analyze, classify, and systematize only these data. Jerold Auerbach quotes a definition of the legal mind given by Thomas Reed Powell of Harvard: it is one that can think of something inexorably connected to something else without thinking about what it is connected to.[10] Such tunnel vision, what Whitehead once called "thought within a groove," obviously gives lawyers great skill in dealing with complex detail. But it does little to develop their social consciousness and concern, and actually helps foster the myth that lawyers are without ideological purpose and have little to do as individuals with the direction society takes.

Legal realism has recently generated a more radical form of itself which is indeed a new development in law's self-understanding: the critical legal studies movement. Begun at Harvard in the 1970s, critical legal theory rejects the notion of law as value free and somehow above political, economic, and social considerations. Critical theorists of this sort insist that law actually embodies the dominant values of society, the ones everyone accepts without question, and only *seems* to be neutral and independent. It therefore tends to lend legitimacy to whatever values and mores predominate at any given time. Like the realists, critical legal theorists presume the instrumentality of law — its use to resolve disputes and produce good social behavior — and focus on the more radical issue of its legitimacy, that is to say, on the validity of a legal system which they see to be part of a structure of power biased toward the rich and always legitimating authority and the values of the status quo. What they want is to give new purpose to law as a social institution, to take the lead in dismantling the various hierarchies of power and privilege which, through the perversion of the legal process, have come to threaten the higher values of our society.[11]

Critical legal theory is thus intent upon unmasking law as just one other form of political power, and understandably it has met with strong resistance on the part of both legal educators and practicing attorneys. But the movement has had the great merit of underlining what legal historians have been saying for some time: law is a creature of society; when society changes, law changes. Law must therefore be understood contextually, not in autonomous isolation as the legal positivists and even the realists tend to think, for such insistence on the uniqueness of law only serves to absolve the legal profession from seeing itself as an inevitable part of a more inclusive pattern of social interaction, responsible for that "firmament of law," to use Robert MacIver's phrase, which represents to the world the life-context of a people.

Hence law must be seen as both product and catalyst of social change, with a capacity to mirror as well as give form to society. Our laws tell us who we are and how we think. Social forces bend the law in one or other direction; law follows these forces and adapts to them. But once changed, law begins to exert its own influence upon events; practices, habits, and customs that are turned into law tend to become stronger, more fixed and more explicit. Law has thus succeeded "in reshaping in less than a generation this nation's views about racism; in altering in even a shorter time police attitudes toward criminal behavior;... in imparting an understanding of poverty;... in stemming religious prejudice; in establishing heightened standards of honesty and public service.... If law can teach, can inculcate, can widen and deepen the nation's humanity, then knowledge of how law works is an indispensable step in using legislation to produce better citizens."[12]

Legal historian Lawrence Friedman has expounded this thesis at some length. "Changes in morals, morality, ways of life," he writes,

> create new demands that press in on legal institutions, including the courts. These institutions then change their behavior or they are pushed and pulled by rival forces. Legal rules, processes and behavior shift.... The new legal situation freezes customs into more solid forms, reinforces certain expectations, sends out new messages, subtly alters culture. It changes ways of thinking and looking at life, the way a prism alters beams of light.

Or again:

> The legal system is not autonomous, not independent of society. It is not a system all to itself.... It is part of the social order, a soldier in the army of society. But its sheer size and presence, its importance, its scale, its interactions with the rest of the social organism give it a meaning beyond that of some limp marionette. Law is society's servant, to be sure. But it is not a quiet, invisible servant in an old-fashioned household; it is the noisy, bumptious work force of a factory.[13]

One could cite many examples of this mutual influence of law and society. The environmental movement, for instance, did not begin inside the legal system. But once it pushed its way into that system, law gave it a new power of enforcement by enacting clean air amendments and specifying endangered species. Social pressures outside the law have likewise modified death penalty statutes. There is general agreement that the death penalty reflects a modern tendency to place much greater reliance on deadly force as a means of overcoming the nation's frustration with crime. Yet such harsher penalties, once solidified into law, inevitably condition for years to come the humane character of our society as well as how we view criminals as persons. In the same way, the so-called medical malpractice crisis is only derivatively a legal crisis and would be inconceivable apart from the revolutionary changes in health care delivery and the ways doctors relate to patients. A certain insensitivity to consumer wants seems to have turned the payer into a purchaser, thereby fueling an expectation of perfection in clinical practice as well as frustration over rising hospital costs. This new aggressiveness then spills over into the courts, which in turn begin to establish a tradition of case law that exerts its own inhibiting power on the medical profession.[14]

Let me end this overview of the relationship between law and American culture with a comment on what Lawrence Friedman has called the "master trend of American legal history." This he understands to be a gradual broadening of the base of the formal system of law, illustrated most dramatically by the civil rights revolution that has dominated our domestic life since the 1950s. Behind this revolution, says Friedman, lies a failure in our egalitarian ideal. We have had, as a consequence, a persistent demand for equality of opportunity, both in law and in fact, on the part of every class of people previously dependent and put down: blacks, women, poor people, homosexuals. Progress in drawing these groups into the ambit of law has been real, but so has public rage and reaction. Arrayed against this movement have been all the hierarchies of power and social distinction historically protected by the very legal system created to establish individual freedom and to guarantee equality.

While the great leap forward by blacks in the 1960s and 1970s symbolizes a shift in this power struggle (which, had it not been for federal courts and federal laws, would surely have been more brutal and violent), the struggle itself goes on. People on the top resent threats to their power and ethical domination; people at the bottom refuse any longer to be docile or deferential. "The basic issue is power," concludes Friedman. "The structural features of the legal system reflect the distribution of power, and, at the same time, influence and perpetuate power.... The result is a delicately balanced system, incredibly complicated, with tremendous tensile strength. Its flaws are also massive; it is tremendously hard to unravel or reform, and it may, at some point, finally rip apart."[15]

2. Religion at the Fault Line

Culture has affected religion in America no less than it has affected law. I have documented elsewhere the religious pluralism that flourished in the colonies when the Founders formulated the religion clauses of the First Amendment.[16] These clauses were conceived as the legal recognition of an actual state of things and as an effort to strengthen the new nation by excluding from government concern all religious differences among its people. The acceptance of religious pluralism meant that Americans gave up the notion, generally accepted at the time, that a government had to use its coercive power to inculcate whatever shared religious belief it thought essential for its wellbeing. This rejection of establishment in favor of persuasion was the single original political ingredient of the new nation. Everything else in the Constitution was either borrowed — separation of powers, bicameral check, federalism — or combined in new ways. But disestablishment was wholly invented. Americans were the first people in history to realize that religious solidarity was not needed to stabilize the social order.

The Founders never interpreted this principle of uncoerced consent to mean that government should be indifferent to religion. The principle meant rather that responsibility for inculcating those truths essential for national stability, generally thought to be common to every religion, rested with the churches alone, to be carried out in whatever ways individual churches wished. This principle was actually an extension into the religious sphere of the key eighteenth-century idea that full consent was the only rational basis for organizing civil government. A mutual independence was thus established: religion was to be safeguarded from the power of the state, and political society was to be safeguarded from interference by organized religion. The immediate gain for the state was the avoidance of political strife along religious lines. But there was also an emphatic affirmation that the religious and political orders were distinct and ought to develop as separate sectors in society. In other words, disestablishment became a legal synonym for secularization, and religious pluralism became its cognitive and cultural corollary.

There was also immediate gain for religion. Law now guaranteed the freedom of every religious group from interference by government as well as by other religious groups. Since no single church was to be established, it was to the self-interest of each to be tolerant of all in order to continue to experience toleration for itself. This meant that the chief characteristic of the churches was their voluntarism. American religion became a "voluntary establishment," to use Elwyn Smith's phrase,[17] with each community competing with all others for allegiance and support. Because the whole strength of an individual church rested upon those people freely consenting to belong to it, its form was usually extremely flexible, reflecting the moods and sentiments of the nation at any given time. Whenever there were shifts in prevailing social attitudes, religious styles and loyalties tended to shift too. Voluntarism thus made religion not only pluralistic but to a certain extent also Protean. It was inevitable that such sensitivity should lead to some confusion regarding the primary religious witness of a particular church, since the essence of pluralism is the multiplication of choice. All churches thus experienced a certain amount of what has been called "cognitive dissonance," anxiety among members who realize the costs involved in having made a certain choice.[18]

Because of this voluntaristic character of their religious institutions Americans began very early to regard religion as a private affair between themselves and their God. This is why they have had such little difficulty reconciling their religious impulses with the results of the secularization process. Both existed in their lives without strain because the vast majority believed that the human enterprise, precisely as human, functions best without explicit reference to religion. Allowing natural reasoning and invention to go as far as they can go, they reasoned, would still leave all the important dimensions of experience to be dealt with by religion, all those larger problems of life and questions of ultimate concern. Politics, science, technology, and economics, in other words, have autonomy in their own spheres and are ruled by their own norms. Martin Marty has called that mentality "religio-secular," a combination of pervasive religiousness and persistent secularity, free from all those profound cultural discontinuities that afflict so many other nations in the West.[19] Institutional religion was thus given a very important but also a very specific role as a Sunday affair. To mention it on weekdays meant that one was expected to speak in terms of values acceptable to the secular mentality of the nation or not to speak at all.

Hence to talk of a "secular humanist conspiracy" in America, as some people do today, is simply silly. What happened over time was that religious people came to hold more or less the same human ideals as people without religion, while at the same time their religiousness became so private and diffused throughout the culture that one sociologist could use the term *invisible* to describe it.[20] Nor were the unreligious secularists necessarily antireligious; most just believed that society was better off when religion was kept privatized. In the public sphere, moreover, both groups looked and acted pretty much the same, because in practice humanism in its theistic form has never been easy to distinguish from its secular form. Both forms agree in valuing personal freedom, tolerance, reason, distributive justice, social discipline, and participation in social decision making. The theists, however, have traditionally been better able to balance the rights of individuals and society by rooting both in God's transcendent purpose and care. Secularists may continue to regard theists with some suspicion, but that is usually because they cannot forget how hard it has been in the past to avoid the risks of bigotry, fanaticism, and obscurantism to which religion has too often been prone.[21]

Unfortunately "secular humanism" has been turned into a scare phrase today by publicists for right-wing fundamentalism. As such, however, it poses very little threat to the majority of religious people, who are themselves already very secular.[22] Humanism divorced from religion is simply another synonym for secularization and modernity. Indeed, its intellectual underpinning is mainly derived from an alliance of the Jewish and Greek traditions—the Greek desire to control the world through human reason, coupled with the Jewish and Christian recognition that history and nature are not in themselves sacred and so can be freed from any immediate dependence on religion. This is why "humanists," whether secular or theist, now dominate the intellectual community in the West, especially the scientific, communications, and educational establishments. What they are propagating is primarily a methodology, namely that the most productive approach to knowledge involves isolation from involvement with any religious institution. There is a problem for religion here only insofar as this secularist methodology is transformed into a worldview and propagated as "secularism," an ideology that seeks to banish all reference to religion as a cultural phenomenon. But again, it is not always easy to distinguish operationally the secular humanist who might hold this ideology from the theistic humanist who rejects it.

Hence the current fundamentalist crusade against "secular humanism" is really a crusade against that modernity with which most Americans generally feel very much at home. This antimodern religious subculture looks back with nostalgia to a more simple, ordered, and homogeneous world where religion is not diffused but highly organized, not tolerant but belligerent. Its members hunger for authority, certainty, unerrancy, and strict moral conformity—in short, for an unpluralistic America unaffected by secularization. They represent a clear-cut, absolutist challenge. Often this challenge is sharply focused, as in the case of abortion, gay rights, pornography, and prayer in public schools. But when it comes to "secular humanism" the focus gets blurred, as in the case of the very odd amendment slipped quietly into the Education for Economic Security Act in 1984. Funds appropriated for magnet schools undertaking desegregation could not be spent, the amendment said, for "any course of instruction the substance of which is secular humanism." Only a half dozen senators seem to have read the measure beforehand, and afterward no one had any idea what they had voted to prohibit. When asked, even Senator Orrin Hatch, the author, could not say what exactly it is that teachers cannot teach.[23]

Another movement in American religion today also seeks to reaffirm life-style boundaries. Like fundamentalism it too can be labeled "sectarian," in the sense of a religious group that resists accommodation to the particular culture in which it finds itself. Unlike fundamentalism it is theologically sophisticated and critical; unlike the old neo-orthodoxy, to which it has most affinity, its conservatism is free of rigidities and open to ecumenical dialogue. Its adherents, however, often referred to as "post-liberal," believe that religion cannot ever really change society and ought not to be in the business of trying. They argue that, since all understandings of right and wrong have to be community based, Christian churches should not presume that they can ever be understood by the secular world. Any effort at all in that direction is doomed from the start and will in addition pose risks to one's religious commitment that Christians should be unwilling to take.

The Christian story, in other words, is irreducibly particular, and can only be heard by those who can speak its biblical language. The "post-liberals" are therefore extremely pessimistic about any effort to reach shared meanings in the secular sphere. This new form of Protestant sectarianism has recently appeared in Roman Catholic form in the Vatican censure of Hans Küng and Charles Curran. Here, however, the issue is the incommunicability of ecclesiastical, not biblical, language. For the Catholic sectarian, theology is a domestic, not a public, undertaking whose natural home is the church, not the academy. Since the purpose of such ecclesiastical language, for the sectarian, is to explain and defend official positions of the Catholic hierarchy, its use to critique these positions (by dialoguing in empathy with modernity) must be rejected as a threat to sectarian identity.[24]

Whether this growth of conservatism and the rising appeal of fundamentalist faith really constitute a "seismic shift" in American religion, as Martin Marty surmises, remains to be seen. If there is indeed such a shift, then it will be because culture-affirming churches fail to realize that their traditionally privatized religion has been responsible not only for diffusing religiousness in America but for diffusing their religious identity as well. Fundamentalists know this well. Modernity indeed serves to focus their identity, but it does so as an enemy, not as a friend. Americans for whom modernity is not the enemy, however, experience a serious and growing need to know who they are religiously. They already have a strong cultural style. What they need is a correspondingly strong spiritual style, a support system to help them successfully bridge the gap between their faith and their culture. This means a macro-morality as well as a micro-morality, an ethics wide-reaching enough to ground their belief in the religious meaning of their secular experience. The *real* danger to mainline religion in America is that it will not develop such a macro-morality, that it will not fight to overcome religious unconcern for the larger problems in society. As we shall see in the next section, there are, nevertheless, persuasive reasons for believing that today a truly "public church" will finally be able to give witness to the social dimension of religious experience.

It is worth noting, here, however, that there are both positive and negative judgments of this ability. On the negative side there is the opinion of sociologist Robert Bellah and his associates that, when the American culture of individualism was carried into the early twentieth century, it was transformed into an ethos holding destructive potential. At that time biblical religion and classical republicanism, both of which were dedicated to public virtue, began to recede in significance, displaced by an expanding utilitarianism of material self-aggrandizement, upon which rest the modern structures of science, technology, and capitalism. In such a cultural atmosphere the historic individualism of religious choice and practice too easily developed into a spirituality of personal self-fulfillment, tailored to private religious taste. To the extent that the self is a person's central spiritual reality, however, moral discussion becomes detached from its social foundation, and church membership is valued as little more than an adventure in self-discovery. Unless this insistent emphasis on self-interest is modified, Bellah says, we shall as citizens develop more and more fragmented lives, and become less and less able to recognize that human happiness must also include involvement in civic life and relationships to others in community.[25]

While Bellah is not optimistic that mainline churches can respond creatively to this situation, he nevertheless sees certain forces acting to restrain individualism's destructive side. These are spelled out in the more positive judgments of another sociologist, Wade Clark Roof. He believes that if voluntarism means anything when applied to American religion, it surely means that the religious symbols of Americans are highly adaptable and resilient, and characterized by tenacity and scrappy independence. For in every major transition period, he says, the complexion of mainline religious institutions underwent something of an alteration, either toward a more prophetic public stance or toward a more accommodating private stance — an alteration that sprang from the changing moods and dispositions of the populace as a whole. The growing intensity of the current debate on such public issues as abortion, homosexuality, and women's place in church and society seems to Roof to indicate that, on matters of ethics and life-styles, these institutions are willing once more to exercise a prophetic and critical function in society.[26]

Hence some doubt still remains regarding the present ability of American churches to articulate socially significant meanings for their particular traditions. One thing is clear, however: these institutional shifts, whether seismic or not, are surface manifestations on the religious landscape of a much larger, underlying spiritual ferment. Disestablishment has meant for the nation a pluralism of religious commitments, with no unifying set of beliefs or ideals held by all. Multiple worldviews and multiple value systems now coexist together in peace. As the legal synonym for secularization, disestablishment has also fostered a privatization of religion and a "religio-secular" mentality that continues to carry with it today a certain degree of destabilization and unresolved ambiguity. If churches retain meaning for their members on a personal level, do they not risk losing it for society at large? But if they manage to be historically relevant to the public realm, might they not cease to respond to the spiritual needs of ordinary people? The aggressiveness of the fundamentalists and their incivility in the civic arena aggravate this dilemma.

Grappling with these questions, however, has also engendered an unusual dynamism in the churches. On the one hand we have the beginnings of a deprivatizing impulse rarely seen in mainline American religion. On the other hand we have religious leaders aware for the first time of the cultural need for religion as an institution to interact with law. It is to this interaction that we now turn. For I believe that in our time the stage is being set for a search on the part of both to find and to articulate the common good.

3. Common Good as Meeting Place

Attempts to describe how religion and law interact in America are a relatively recent phenomenon. The reason is that, from the time the new nation was founded, religious institutions were generally convinced that their most important public role consisted in exercising the freedom guaranteed them by law to believe, teach, and worship as they chose. As we saw already, in exercising this freedom each church accepted its exercise also by every other church, thereby acknowledging the right of all citizens to be nourished religiously in any way they wished. The resulting pluralism not only individualized religious membership but also privatized religious experience. To guarantee that government would not interfere with such privacy, religious bodies were scrupulous on their part not to interfere with government. Thus the more distinctive the doctrine and morals of a particular church, the less relevant they were thought to be in the public realm. Only beliefs and morality commonly held by all churches could easily provide a practical basis for social life, and when these entered the public sphere they were usually given voice not by religious leaders but by officials of the state.

There may be a deeper reason in our history, however, for religious institutions as such interacting so infrequently with law. American religion was predominantly Protestant, and Protestantism, as Peter Berger has observed, is characterized by "an immense shrinkage in the scope of the sacred." Reality for the Protestant "is polarized between a radically transcendent divinity and a radically 'fallen' humanity that, *ipso facto*, is devoid of sacred qualities. Between them lies an altogether 'natural' universe, God's creation to be sure, but in itself bereft of numinosity. In other words, the radical transcendence of God confronts a universe of radical immanence, of 'closedness' to the sacred. Religiously speaking, the world becomes very lonely indeed." [27]

Though Berger's comments perhaps describe the outlook of Lutherans more than that of other Protestants, every Protestant tradition nevertheless has elements of this dualism. To the degree it is present, says H. Richard Niebuhr, it has tended "to lead Christians into antinomianism and into cultural conservatism." They have been "deeply concerned to bring change into only one of the great cultural institutions—the religious. For the rest they seemed to be content to let state and economic life...continue relatively unchanged." Laws were consequently seen as restraining forces, "dykes against sin, preventers of anarchy, rather than as positive agencies through which men in social union render positive service to neighbors advancing toward true life." [28]

This lack of interaction between religion and law in the past fostered unfortunate presuppositions within both insitutions. Religious people usually made the mistake of presuming that church-state separation, or the separation of legal and religious institutions, had to be reflected in a separation of religious and legal values as well as in the total secularization of legal thought. The corollary of this mistake was another: the failure to distinguish between public order on the one hand, reflecting the coercive aspects of law, and the common good on the other hand, entrusted both to law and to other institutions, an arena where they all interact with each other in a context of pluralism and free public debate.

The legal mind had its own presuppositions. It found it

extremely difficult, for example, to distinguish moral values from moral absolutes. For positivists, genuinely shared meanings in public life could be reached only by fiat. Hence the entry of religious groups into the civic arena was always equated with an effort to impose some religious policy. In the positivist mind this presented a special danger to government, since by law there was no way to control what any religious group believed and taught. Disestablishment and pluralism thus tended to inhibit both law and religion from even discussing values and commitments that could be shared together in the public sphere.

Much has happened in recent years to change this. As we have seen, both institutions are now in a cultural transition. Law, for example, is becoming aware that issues of justice and equality, which face it on every side, are much more than questions of fair procedure; they involve value choices and moral commitments on the part of the nation as a whole. Our great conscience problem today is the conflict between our genuine egalitarian tradition, on the one hand, and the anti-egalitarianism of our economic system on the other hand. Civil rights, human rights, and economic rights have consequently become the leitmotif of growing litigation in the courts.

Federal and state legislatures, for example, grapple daily with issues like the right to health care. Many in the past were puzzled at the whole concept of such a "right," since it was taken for granted until very recently that health care was a privilege. Unlike the negative promotion required by rights like freedom of expression (achieved simply by noninterference), the right to health care, if it is affirmed for all citizens, demands very positive promotion, a social cooperation of a very high degree on the part of multiple agencies in the nation. This means the need for legislation that will equitably distribute the economic burden of health care through the whole of society, rather than impose it upon a few agencies. Moral discourse is thus finding its way back into legal discourse at the very time that religious discourse is becoming less privatized and more sensitive to promotion of the common good. This latter development is perhaps the more significant, because in any interaction between law and religion, it is religion which must necessarily take the initiative.

I think there are three reasons why religious institutions have become more conscious of their responsibility for the common good. First, while they have traditionally had little difficulty with institutional pluralism, they have recently been finding it increasingly difficult to support the contemporary spread of moral pluralism. Until the present generation, a broad consensus on public morality seems to have characterized American life. However secularized it had become, however dependent upon the patronage of public officials, this broad consensus was always presumed to be there, and to be able to survive without a sectarian base. *Roe v. Wade* challenged both assumptions. The abortion question made it clear that the issue is no longer that of morality verus immorality, but of two sharply differentiated moral positions, each articulated in terms of fundamental individual rights, each consistent in its own way with America's individualist ethos. Under the guise of being value-neutral, the Supreme Court in *Wade* edicted into law value judgments that were in fact alien to the religious tradition that had historically grounded public morals. More than anything in recent history, the abortion cases taught religious people that moral disputes were going to be referred more and more to the judicial and political processes, and that their involvement in these processes was imperative, since they now functioned as sources for a common binding morality.

A second reason for greater religious sensitivity to the common good has been a widespread recovery of the prophetic tradition.[29] This tradition has always been operative in American religion, though most often at its periphery. It begins to move toward the center as soon as some concrete social structure is clearly seen to deny justice to a certain segment of society. This was the case when strong religious support was enlisted for the abolition of slavery in the nineteenth century and for the growth of labor unions in the early twentieth. The tradition fell into decline, however, and remained so until rekindled in the 1960s by Martin Luther King's prophetic call to end racial segregation and to recognize the dignity of all black Americans. Today the tradition is making itself felt strongly again: in the sanctuary movement for those fleeing oppression in Latin America; in the advocacy of civil rights for homosexuals and equal rights for women; in denunciation of the nuclear arms race, hard-core pornography, and capital punishment; in national efforts to arouse concern for the plight of the poor, the homeless, and the elderly. Along with movements on both sides of the abortion question, all these foci of economic and social justice involve law. As a result, advocates of the tradition are finding themselves constantly calling upon law to assert its civic and social responsibility.

A third reason for religion's current focus on the common good is theological: a growing conviction on the part of many that God's creative and salvific action must be present somehow in all human experience, whether secular or sacred. Looked at in this way, no human institution, however sinful, is an autonomous structure in which God has no interest, since every human institution influences the way people live in society, which in turn influences the way they think about God and their neighbor. The fact that secular institutions are never found to be all good, that most are indeed ambiguous, a mix of good and bad, some very bad, is simply a reflection of the human condition.

The prior concern of the religious person, therefore, is not what she or he should be doing in secular life but what God might be doing. For before any individual pursues human development, God pursues it. Before any individual promotes freedom and equality, God does. Nor is this to imply that human institutions can ever escape frustration and even subversion from human sinfulness. It is simply to assert that they are human and as such objects of a divine will. Though ultimately the purpose of God's providential design is salvific, the union of all persons with God's own self in the sphere of the sacred, God's immediate creative purposes in the secular must be secular, i.e., in conformity with the nature of any given institution. These purposes may be shrouded in mystery, but they are carried out nonetheless through the meshing of divine providence with human prudence, through the instrumentality of men and women whose prudential judgments in the secular world further any given providential design. History is thus not simply a course of human events, but a series of dramatic encounters between the human and divine.[30]

Religion's sharpened focus upon the common good has been paralleled, as I said, by a developing sense of social responsibility on the part of law. While the legal profession has always functioned to some extent as an interactive structure in society, able to influence life in business, government, and local communities, the fact is that legal positivists and realists have never felt at home with concepts like "the common good." While their highly individualistic professionalism argued for law's value neutrality, their skepticism usually looked upon morals as no more than officially established mores. This moral aloofness, however, has been receding for some time. As we saw earlier, every class of people has now been brought into the ambit of law. In the face of the nation's moral pluralism, value choices for the larger society have gradually come to be synonymous with legal choices. The reason is that whenever customary norms break down, Americans always turn to law, forcing it to fill the vacuum. As other authorities weaken, law by default assumes a commanding importance, the final way out of dilemmas stemming from moral as well as political controversy. For in courts most questions get answers, and most decisions get respect.

But this respect is often given grudgingly, accompanied by a deep resentment of law's power to control. This is because, as one distinguished jurist admits, American attitudes toward law "make up a history of fierce and unresolved tension."[31] Americans are likely to shift between an uncritical trust in what law can accomplish to an excessive mistrust, between an extreme legalism that accepts law and morals as one, and an equally extreme antilegalism rooted in either disillusionment or moral absolutism. Hence the paradox today is that in spite of law's ever-expanding horizon, and the willingness of courts to make value judgments on social and economic questions, there is a crisis in law's authority that will not subside. Harold Berman believes that, unlike earlier times, the nation is threatened today not by the worship of law but by contempt for it. Our problem with law is not fear but disillusionment.[32]

Why should this be so? Because law, for all its influence upon society, remains a creature of society. Karl Llewellyn once said that lawyers mirror undistorted the very society that accuses them of social irresponsibility.[33] This explains the current defensiveness of the professional bar, especially in the wake of Watergate, and its frequent emphasis on "law reform."[34] Such reform, mainly through a proliferation of books on lawyers' ethics and revisions in the Code of Professional Responsibility, is a response to the beleaguered comradeship of the profession's elite, as well as an effort to show the world that lawyers still really do serve the public interest.[35] These surface phenomena, however, point not to a crisis in law so much as to the deeper crisis in American society, and the naming of this crisis, suggests Douglas Sturm, is ultimately an expression of religious sensibility. "American society has been organized," he writes, "to honor the principle of individualism.... The crisis which gives rise to concern for the future of American public life is centered in the inability of the principle of individualism as it has been embodied in the institutions and consciousness of American society to ground and to support a genuinely public life as needed at this point of history."[36]

The conclusion of one important sociological study is that the chief source of this crisis is a language problem: we have lost the ability to speak to one another in a public way about community values and public moral goods. As a nation we once had languages that enabled us to do this, a biblical language emphasizing just and compassionate social structures, and a republican language concerned with civic responsibility and community service. While these languages are still latent in our cultural memory, we have unwittingly displaced them in public conversation by our current vocabulary of personal self-fulfillment and financial success. Unless we can retrieve these languages, therefore, and make them usable again, we shall be without the necessary means to discern those new meanings of community and common good proper to our particular age.[37]

But are these languages from our past compatible with the language of rights and freedom that we believe so central to our contemporary experience? While some have lost all hope of finding such compatibility,[38] many others are coming to believe that it can indeed be found, provided that in our search no one of pluralism's many goods is absolutized or allowed to dominate the others.[39] In other words, the place of each must be recognized and respected in the framework of social existence. We may as a result no longer be able to appeal to some absolute standard of goodness, but our gain shall be to guarantee to each person the right to participate in the total life of the community. From this perspective all rights, including one's legal rights, can be seen as having a communitarian as well as an individualistic character; an orientation toward a limited but nonetheless real agreement on the good, not simply a protection against the coercive behavior of one's fellows. Jeffrey Stout has made this point well:

> The idea that society lacks any shared conception of the good is false, but that does not mean that all is well. It could still be the case that politics, as the social practice of self-governance directed toward the common good, has begun to give way to merely bureaucratic management of competition for external goods. It is therefore right to worry about becoming despots and barbarians. On the other hand, the social practice of politics is *always* being threatened in some way. All genuine republics, not just the liberal kind, are fragile things, susceptible to corruption by external goods.[40]

4. The Burden of Conversation

The stage has been set, then. What we have at present is a national love-hate relationship with law, generating a growing attempt in legal circles to deal more responsibly with the larger needs of society. At the same time various dynamisms have been operative in religious institutions to overcome their privatism and the moral anomie of their pluralism. This effort of churches to generate positive values for common action inevitably moves them into the ambit of public policy and law. Within this ambit, however, interrelationships can never be smooth, because religion and law both share that culture of individualism so deeply imbedded in the American psyche. This legacy of secularization, embraced by theist and nontheist alike, will always make it difficult to find shared meanings and to articulate values related to the common good. But the difficult is not the impossible. A sign of encouragement is that both legal people and religious people, each in their own way, have begun to recognize the existence of the problem. A new phase in their relationship seems to be developing wherein both are trying to develop strategies and to support public commitments that are larger than individual preferences. Both are now searching for some new social ethic, for ways to understand anew what is right and wrong for the community as a whole.[41]

One can, of course, speak more easily of religion's *indirect* impact upon the public sphere, through its influence in shaping the perspectives and nurturing the values of individual women and men. Such influence is quite consistent with the "religio-secular" mentality described earlier. One's religious beliefs concerning the larger questions of life necessarily generate ethical imperatives that in turn infiltrate public thought, thereby shaping those social structures in which a particular person lives. In this indirect sense religion in America has never been and will never be irrelevant to law or public policy. A conviction that social structures and secular enterprises function best without explicit reference to institutional religion does not mean that such structures and enterprises are free of influence from religious values. If asked, the majority of Americans would probably identify their most important values as in fact religion-based, and even those who do not would have little difficulty recognizing the role of religion in the lives of Americans around them. This is clearly what de Toqueville meant when he called religion "the first of their political institutions."[42] Neither he nor anyone else at the time could possibly have conceived churches intervening as institutions in public life. What churches were supposed to do was rather to safeguard the moral standards of their members and to facilitate the use of their political freedom, thereby producing citizens whose character was especially ready to influence law and public policy by promoting peace, order, and justice.

In contrast to this indirect influence, what we are dealing with here is the direct and formal intervention by churches precisely as institutions. I think that two issues have to be faced. The first is this: what are the questions that should focus these initiatives in the public realm? This issue is so important because most of these questions will presuppose some legal strategy in their answers. But if law is indeed a tool of society, the danger is that religion, which in this country has tended to keep its distance from law, will now go from no use to bad use. For it must not be forgotten that, in countries where it has been established, Christianity has had a long history of relying on law to promote its own particular interests, ignore interests of minorities, and block any secular challenge to its authority. Hence if there is to be any true religious concern for the public weal in this country, churches must first be extremely sensitive to all indicators of public need. If, for example, America's individualism is slowly draining the nation both of commonly shared meanings and of a language to articulate community values, would this not indicate that questions raised by religious institutions ought to focus on meanings which in principle can be shared by everyone? Would these not be the meanings more likely to be invested by law with creative possibilities for social justice?

Judged on this standard, prayer in public schools would hardly qualify as one of these questions. This very narrow sectarian response obviously masks a more general fear that the nation as a whole no longer cherishes certain religious traditions. The ugliness of the debate engendered, however, as well as its approach to law, does little either to advance these traditions or to reduce hostility to religion. The same problem arises from attempts to pass laws requiring the teaching of "creation science." This is really an effort to deal with a much deeper problem, an educational outlook that aims to teach students about life in America with textbooks that read as if religion hardly exists. Such an ideology may indeed be operative in certain educational circles, but trying to combat it by injecting into public schools vacuous prayer or spurious data on the age of the earth is simply to oppose one ideology with another. The whole effort has nothing to do with public discussion and in fact testifies to a loss of confidence in such discussion, as does every other attempt at single issue politics, from denouncements of abortion to campaigns against the rights of women and homosexuals. These issues are raised in public not because questions are thought to be open, offering hope of creative answers and shared meanings, but because they are presumed to be closed to all consideration of change.

In contrast to such narrow sectarian questions are questions that can be resolved neither by the power of the state nor in the confines of particular communities. It is by stressing the importance of these questions that the true role of religion to strengthen society will be found. For such questions are genuinely public, as opposed to purely political, and they will rely initially upon law mainly to prevent closure before their meanings can be shared and creative answers developed. "Questions for which we are convinced there is no answer," says Robin Lovin, "are as closed as questions for which only one answer is allowed."[43] The consequence, however, is that in many areas, such as the legal and moral aspects of abortion, we may have to live for some time without any genuine public consensus. This apparent inability to bring public debate to satisfactory resolution has lead to judgments like that of Alasdair MacIntrye that the whole effort should be abandoned. For him, unless there can be consensus on everything, there can be consensus on nothing; unless a community shares a single vision there can only be moral chaos, "civil war carried out by other means."[44] He is appalled at the fragmentation of moral norms, but his pessimism contributes little to the creation of shared meanings by simply deploring the pluralism that is the source of the problem.

This brings us to the second issue to be faced by churches that now stand ready to influence public policy: given the type of open question to be asked, how is the discussion of possible shared meanings to be carried out? Obviously the point of departure must be some biblical or ecclesiastical base, since we are talking about initiatives by religious people striving to be faithful to the vision and values of their own community. Public consensus, however, either with other religious groups or with judicial and legislative bodies, can never develop unless the proposals for shared meanings are publicly accessible, that is to say, intelligible apart from the particular religious experience that was their origin. This does not mean that such origins are to be denied, or that the specificity of a religious tradition is to be eliminated from the ethical dialogue, but only that, in a pluralist society, these origins and specificities cannot be advanced to vouch for the truth of any specific institutional claim.

Nor is there question here of divesting oneself of one's religious language; the issue is rather how, through reason and community experience, to translate such language into terms accessible to those outside one's tradition. Remember that we are talking here about how to achieve consensus on civic action, not consensus on religious belief. "What is required," says Robin Lovin, "is a criterion of public truth that is different from the criterion for a correct interpretation of one's own tradition, a criterion that requires corroboration of one's claims in the critical scrutiny of another community of meaning and which holds back from claims to this sort of truth until the corroboration is forthcoming."[45] In the short run, of course, this process will make easy agreements difficult, not only because religious communities will disagree with each other, but also because their convictions will both overlap and run counter to the prevailing convictions of secular culture.

Kent Greenawalt has studied in depth this issue of including religious communities in public discourse. He prefaces his guidelines for such inclusion with four optimistic assumptions: that there is now in the United States a substantial consensus on the organizing political principles for society; that there exists a shared sense that major political discussions will be carried on primarily in secular terms; that most people respect religious belief and hesitate to attack religious practice as nonsensical; that it is possible to be at one and the same time a seriously religious person and a liberal participant in a liberal society. His conclusion is that "an individual acts consistently with the spirit of political liberalism when, adopting a position on an issue of public policy, he gives weight to his religious convictions." When speaking to an audience of those who do not share his religious premises, "he should ordinarily cast his arguments in essentially nonreligious terms, though he should not conceal the bases of his own convictions and should feel free to use cultural imagery that derives from our religious tradition."[46]

The advantages of such civil argument are not to be underestimated. Perhaps the most important advantage is that religious groups will inevitably tend to become more realistic about the consequences of disestablishment and pluralism. For it is the very nature of a secularized society like the United States to be complex and contradictory in regard to shared meanings. Precisely because such a society does not respond to any single organizing principle, the differences between religious and legal values will always lack the rigidity implied by terms like "separation of church and state" and "autonomy of the secular." Hence religious readings of social reality are much more likely to be met with sharp critique than with passive tolerance. On the other hand, while indifference does not characterize our national outlook on religion, ambivalence does, and this naturally renders suspect all attempts to relate shared meanings too easily to moral imperatives, much less to the will of God. There can thus be no simple or completely stable relationship between religion and law, even though in a given case the dialogue and its results may be quite satisfying for both. Each institution has to adapt to the other, and the initiative in such mutual adaptation must almost always come from religion.

Such initiatives can never be successful, however, if religious people come to the public dialogue with values prepackaged in sectarian bundles, to be taken or left by the other participants, and with little concern that these values may be offending legal sensitivities or moral judgments already in place. Churches generally have had little practice in avoiding either mistake. This is the reason that institutional religion has at times in our history functioned as a social solvent rather than as a binding force. When it interacts with law, therefore, religion needs to be patient, since shared meanings result initially not so much from public analysis and argument as from a certain cultural experience that develops deep in the national psyche.

Often much time is needed for a people to discover that something is wrong with their culture, as in the slow recognition of the injustice of racial segregation and the need to enact laws to combat it. Religion must indeed be involved in all such public efforts to dispel illusion and come to new moral insight and choice. But such involvement is important not because religion has any monopoly on morals, but rather because public choices on how to be human have to be guarded from superficiality. Before embracing laws and shared meanings, Americans have traditionally sought first to root them in God's transcendent purpose and care. They will finally give their allegiance only when they perceive that such laws and meanings are not in fact superficial and do indeed satisfy these deeper spiritual needs.

Let me briefly summarize what I have said about religion and law in American life. My central point has been that the peculiar history of these two institutions and their response to cultural change have brought them both in our time to a heightened sensitivity and awareness of the common good. Hence the capacity of each to interact with the other is now high. Both recognize that our society is being threatened by a breakdown of consensus on issues central to our survival: nuclear war, environmental decay, civil rights, growing poverty and homelessness, population control, abortion, pornography, the functioning of the capitalistic system. In searching for new shared meanings, however, religion has to take the initiative; disestablishment means that law can never on its own move in religion's direction. Will such initiatives actually take place on any large scale, and if they do, will they work? It all depends on whether culture-affirming churches can articulate a macro-morality that is intelligible apart from church origins, while at the same time not losing sight of those specific religious identities which nourish the spirituality of church members. Fundamentalist communities, of course, relatively untouched by modernity, know nothing of this double task.

I think it important to emphasize, by way of conclusion, that I do not believe that an ideology hostile in principle to public religious initiative any longer exists in as virulent a form as some would claim.[47] Religion is simply too pervasive and diffuse in our social milieu; too many of our cultural assumptions are seen today as involving beliefs which transcend our native pragmatism. In other words, secularization as a human process and methodology is not to be confused with secularism as a worldview. I also believe that secularization as a social fact has been an enormous boon to humankind. It opposes religion not *qua* religion but *qua* control system. It is not religion which is the problem in the public sphere but the rigidities of a fundamentalist mentality, whether its origins be biblical or ecclesiastical. For society's control system is now no longer religion but law. Because law correlates with social change, however, and social change with shared moral values, law will always have to respond to religion as principal carrier of values. This response has become so problematic in our time because America's endemic individualism is now bringing with it a degree of moral pluralism unacceptable to law as well as to religion. And this is why their interaction has now become that of equals and is generally accepted today as both inevitable and necessary.

Yet it would be foolish to believe that no compromises will have to be made, since historically the discovery of the common good has been the primary focus of neither institution. Even in the best of scenarios, therefore, their interaction will never be free of conflict nor secure against the demands of rival moral claims. This is a hard saying for Americans. Political analyst Mona Harrington has shown that as a nation we are attached to a long-standing myth: "the conviction that human relations are, by their nature, harmonious, that *serious* conflict in human societies is unnatural and unnecessary." Hence differences of interest among different groups, while inevitable, are seen as essentially superficial, for deep beneath such contention there exists "a beneficent natural order within which all interests are complimentary." As a people we seem to believe that relatively simple adjustments are all that is needed to "resolve conflict *without loss to any legitimate interest.*"[48]

The positive value of such public conflicts, however, is to be found not in their easy resolution but in their capacity to be creative of fresh moral insight. For this to happen, as Reinhold Niebuhr often reminded us, we have to recognize that the root source of these conflicts is our endemic capacity as human beings to abuse and turn to evil every fresh possibility for good. Such negative capacity can never be eliminated but only controlled. This is the reason, said Niebuhr, that the Constitution has so many built-in safeguards against the accumulation of power: its framers believed in original sin.

> All social cooperation on a larger scale than the most intimate social group requires a measure of coercion. . . . Politics will, to the end of history, be an area where conscience and power meet, where the ethical and coercive factors of human life will interpenetrate and work out their tentative and uneasy compromises. . . . A too uncritical glorification of cooperation and mutuality therefore results in the acceptance of traditional injustices and the preference of the subtler types of coercion to the more overt types.[49]

Nevertheless, Niebuhr's life-long belief that public conflicts can never be completely resolved was provisional, not final. For he also believed that there are indeterminate possibilities for good on the human scene, and that, historically, our human capacity for justice is what produced America's democracy. "There are no limits to be set in history for the achievement of more universal brotherhood, for the development of more perfect and more inclusive mutual relations."[50] What he would surely say is that all parties involved must be willing to adjust their prior claims in the light of the public argument and wise enough to recognize the difference between what can and cannot be changed. Religious institutions especially have to remember that what they are seeking in the public sphere is consensus on civic action, not consensus on religious belief, and that in certain cases this cannot be achieved without loss of some legitimate interest. Stubborn commitment on their part to only one possible outcome could mean that a particular conflict cannot be creative at all and that new possibilities for the community can never be realized.

PART II
THE RIDDLE OF THE ESTABLISHMENT CLAUSE

IN JULY 1985 EDWIN MEESE 3rd did a curious thing for an attorney general of the United States. He attacked the Supreme Court. In an address to the American Bar Association that summer he castigated the Court for not properly performing its duty to interpret the Constitution and called upon it to adopt what he called a "jurisprudence of original intention." He criticized it especially for its recent decisions in the area of religion. These were examples, he said, of ignoring the intent of the framers and following the policy preferences of individual justices. Those who wrote the religion clauses of the First Amendment, he insisted, would find the Court's doctrine of "strict neutrality between religion and non-religion... somewhat bizarre." In an undelivered portion of his text, Meese also asserted that the Court had been on intellectually shaky ground these last sixty years in reading the Fourteenth Amendment to apply to the states key provisions of the Bill of Rights. Without such application, he implied, states would be free to ignore federal restrictions on establishment and to aid religion in any way they chose.

Two Supreme Court justices lost no time in responding to this attack. Justice William J. Brennan, Jr., called such an outlook "facile historicism." It "feigns self-effacing deference" to the framers but "in truth is little more than arrogance cloaked as humility." It is arrogant, he continued, "to pretend that from our vantage we can gauge accurately the intent of the framers on application of principles to specific contemporary questions. Apart from the problematic nature of the sources, our distance of two centuries cannot but work as a prism refracting all we perceive." Justice John Paul Stevens's response discussed Meese by name. He said that "the Attorney General fails to mention the fact that no Justice who has sat on the Supreme Court during the past sixty years has questioned" the applicability of the First Amendment to state governments. "The development of his argument is somewhat incomplete," continued Stevens, "because its concentration on the original intention of the framers of the Bill of Rights overlooks the importance of subsequent events in the development of our law." One year later Justice Byron White registered his own opinion on the subject, saying that "this Court does not subscribe to the simplistic view that constitutional interpretation can possibly be limited to the 'plain meaning' of the Constitution's text or to the subjective intention of the framers."[1]

What we are witnessing in these exchanges is the public outbreak at a particular time of a perennial dispute on constitutional interpretation. The issue is a vexing one in constitutional law generally, but in recent years it has become particularly troublesome in regard to the establishment clause of the First Amendment. The attorney general's critique and the justices' responses are symptomatic of widespread and growing national debate on this clause, its original meaning, its history, and especially the role of the Supreme Court in applying it to contemporary situations. By contrast, the free exercise clause of the same amendment has never really caused much difficulty, probably because religious liberty has been so much part of our ethos of freedom from the start, accepted everywhere as an unavoidable corollary of our religious pluralism. The establishment clause, however, has always been problematic and its interpretation inseparable from the changing role of religion in society.

The Riddle of the Establishment Clause 39

The establishment clause has, as we shall see, all the earmarks of a riddle. No area of modern constitutional law has been so beset with sectarian aspiration and tension or so productive of judicial discord and strife. What the Founders thought and said and meant is only half the story, perhaps less than half. The full story up to the present is far more complex and ambiguous, posing questions to which there are no simple answers but whose asking nevertheless pushes the story into a future as yet only dimly perceived.

Before we begin this story, a preliminary observation is in order. The religion clauses of the First Amendment do not deal with the role of religion in American society but only with its legal disestablishment and its guaranteed free exercise vis-à-vis government. The distinction between government and society is therefore critical to any discussion of these clauses. Government is that part of society concerned with the maintenance of public order through law and its enforcement, as well as with the administration of public affairs both domestic and foreign. Society is that much larger entity embracing all the various communities of human life: families, religious and educational institutions, businesses great and small, all voluntary associations and social organizations, as well as all political activity, including governance. Government promotes the common good by establishing peace and justice in society; society in and through its various components seeks the common good in a larger sense, namely, whatever meets the spiritual, moral, and material needs of all its people.

"Religion and government" is therefore a far more accurate phrase in the American context than "church and state." The latter is wholly European in origin and occasions almost the only American use of *state* as a substantive in the sense of "government." Europeans speak of permanent "states" and changing "governments"; we speak of a permanent government and changing political leaders. We normally use *state* to signify one of our fifty geographic entities, each with its "state government." The phrase "church and state" also contains the uncommon abstract use of *church*. In this country *religion* is the more common abstract term, with *church* referring ordinarily to various concrete religious denominations. While "religion and government" may lack classical status and historic overtones, it speaks with much greater accuracy to the phenomenon as it exists in the United States.[2]

Beginning, then, the story of the establishment clause, I shall trace it through its several historical segments. First we shall see what the Founders thought and said about disestablishment and how the various churches functioned in America following the enactment of the First Amendment. Next we shall examine the major revision of the Founders' legacy, wrought in principle by the Fourteenth Amendment in 1868 and in practice by the Supreme Court beginning in 1925, as well as how this major revision was affected by the changing role of religion in the 1940s and 1950s and by the turbulence of the 1960s and 1970s. Finally we shall note the reconsideration and compromise that we may expect to find in the relationship between religion and government in the years and decades ahead. In each of these segments key problems of interpretation emerge and the reader will become aware of how complex are the issues involved. The conclusion I will draw at the end of the story is that interpreting the establishment clause will very likely constitute no less a riddle in our third century than it has for us up to the present.

1. The Founders' Disestablishment

The Problem of Original Intention

How did the Founders think about government's relation to religion? To seek an answer to this question is to unravel the extraordinary variety in the ways religion was regarded at the time of the Revolution and during the years immediately preceding the Constitution of 1787. It

The Riddle of the Establishment Clause   41

is also to expose the multiple and finally unsolvable ambiguities connected with the wording, and therefore with the meaning, of the First Amendment. The thought of Jefferson and Madison is most often cited to explain the intent of the religion clauses. (The Supreme Court in its early decisions on establishment repeatedly refers to these two statesmen.) But Jefferson had nothing at all to do with the clauses; he was not even in the country at the time the Constitution was debated or the Bill of Rights hammered out, and his famous "wall of separation" metaphor did not appear in his writings until over a decade later. Madison was indeed a chief architect of both the Constitution and Bill of Rights, but the language of the First Amendment, though certainly not uncongenial to him, was very possibly not his work at all. So we need to look more closely.

Bernard Bailyn has documented with admirable clarity what he calls the "contagion of liberty" that swept America and infected all areas of colonial life. Indeed, as he says, "the fear of a comprehensive conspiracy against liberty... lay at the heart of the Revolution."[3] It was therefore taken for granted that the purpose of all constitutions in the colonies was to specify and protect inalienable rights and to limit the ordinary actions of government. The suspicion of every type of political power not derived from the people inevitably became a suspicion of ecclesiastical power also, since that too represented a form of coercion, the dominion of some people over others.

Only in the case of slavery did this challenge to dominion falter, for economic reasons, and finally fail, though even here the "contagion of liberty" exposed the contradiction in all its ugliness and prompted even statesmen from the southern colonies to look forward to a time when "this lamentable evil" could be abolished. Madison's sad words at the Constitutional Convention anticipated the arguments of moderates a generation later: "Great as the evil is, a dismemberment of the union would be worse."[4] Churchly power, however, had no such economic protection from the "logic of Revolutionary thought." Bailyn notes how weak and ill-defined were the establishments in the various colonies, yet they came under fire nevertheless, both from sectarians, who wanted freedom *for* their sects, and from political idealists, inspired by the rationalism of the Enlightenment, who wanted freedom *from* these same sects.

The sectarians, also referred to as "dissenters," were the Baptists, the largest in number and the most vocal, the Quakers, and many Methodists and Presbyterians. They tended to see all government negatively, as mainly coercive in character, and believed in the complete separation of religion as the highest manifestation of their liberty as Christians. The movement's early leaders, Roger Williams and William Penn, created in Rhode Island and Pennsylvania something totally new at the time, colonies without establishments. Later, when the Constitution was written, Baptist leaders like John Leland of Virginia and Isaac Backus of Massachusetts wanted freedom as a right, not as a favor from weak state establishments. Their movement's acute individualism and religious impulse of withdrawal accorded well with the civic individualism of the "enlightened," and it was, as Bailyn says, "touched by the magic of the Revolutionary thought" and transformed.[5]

Jefferson and Madison were both "enlightened" and as such viewed religion instrumentally, as very much a private affair of conscience and opinion but something nevertheless very useful for the promotion of civic virtue. Jefferson believed that any truths about God and the universe could be known by rational examination of nature alone, without need of any divine revelation, and this conviction he distilled in what he regarded as second in his writings only to the Declaration of Independence, Virginia's "Act for Establishing Religious Freedom." Religious liberty meant the absence of government coercion: "our civil rights have no dependence on our religious opin-

The Riddle of the Establishment Clause   43

ions any more than our opinions in physics and geometry."[6]

Madison, who was influenced by the Anglicanism of his youth and, as a student at Princeton, much more by the Presbyterianism of John Witherspoon, seems to have held beliefs more profound and complex than those of Jefferson and clearly not as opposed to the concept of revealed religion. Yet he was nevertheless an adamant foe of establishment. Faced with a 1785 proposal in the Virginia House of Delegates for a three pence tax to provide for religion teachers, he wrote his "Memorial and Remonstrance Against Religious Assessments" which gave his reason for this opposition: establishment had meant coercion in the past, and it was therefore a violation of basic human freedom to require anyone to support a religious undertaking. "Distant as [the tax] may be in its present form from the Inquisition, it differs from it only in degree."[7]

The non-involvement of government in religious matters was, therefore, the principle defended by Jefferson and Madison throughout their lives. This they did primarily to protect freedom of conscience and to extinguish, as Madison wrote Jefferson, "the ambitious hope of making laws for the human mind."[8] But they both also wanted to promote the freedom of religious practice, in Jefferson's case because he saw that such practice promoted good citizenship, in Madison's case because he also saw it as a bulwark to strengthen religious belief. Hence their principle of separation was not an absolute, all-inclusive prohibition but could be accommodated on occasion to advance political and perhaps also, for Madison, religious ends.

As governor of Virginia, Jefferson drafted a "Bill for Appointing Days of Public Fasting and Thanksgiving" (introduced by Madison in the Virginia legislature) that required all ministers to preach on these occasions, and he did not hesitate to invoke "nature's God" in the Declaration of Independence and in his second inaugural address as president. For his part, Madison raised no constitutional objection in Congress, less than two months after the First Amendment became effective, to government support of a chaplaincy system, and, as president during the War of 1812, he issued four proclamations recommending public days of prayer and fasting, though much later in his life he considered both actions to have been ill-advised. But that was because, as he wrote a friend in 1832, "it may not be easy, in every possible case, to trace the line of separation between the rights of religion and the Civil authority with such distinctness as to avoid collisions and doubts on unessential points."[9]

This effort of Madison to avoid collisions in the religious area appears clearly in the *Federalist Papers*, where in numbers 10 and 51 he captured perfectly that suspicion of power which, as we saw earlier, was the dominant political ethos of the time. He specifically mentions religion as one of the causes of competing "factions," groups seeking to advance their narrow private concerns. These factions, he says, are inevitable in a free government, and the aim of a separation of powers in the new Constitution should be not to harmonize but to neutralize them, thereby enabling enlightened elected leaders more easily to perceive and promote the common good. In No. 51 Madison finds in religion the analogy for this realistic pluralist stance. "In a free government the security for civil rights must be the same as that for religious rights. It consists in the one case in the multiplicity of interests, and in the other in the multiplicity of sects. The degree of security in both cases will depend on the number of interests and sects."[10]

Madison would surely not deny that the "sects" also had concerns common to all; he was focusing his analogy rather on their capacity to coerce. As William Lee Miller perceptively remarks, "The protection of religious liberty, he now saw, was to be found not only in declarations of rights, in principles and convictions, or even in laws; it was to be found also in a power situation — a division and balance — in which the numbers of, and conflicts among, religious groups made overbearing combinations unlikely."[11] Religious freedom could be guaranteed in the expectation that religious observance would flourish and with it morality and restraint in public life. But these benefits would be realized only if religious pluralism was also guaranteed and all monopoly in religion avoided.

It is scarcely possible to overestimate this combined influence of sectarians and the "enlightened" on the enactment of the religion clauses of the First Amendment. Nevertheless, five states still had establishments when the First Congress began discussing a bill of rights in 1789, and their representatives wanted nothing in the clauses which would jeopardize these establishments. To complicate matters more, many delegates were Federalists, who, like Madison himself, believed that the Constitution had no need to provide for the protection of individual rights at all. These, they held, were already guaranteed by the fact that actions of the federal government were limited to what the Constitution explicitly allowed, and since the Constitution granted no power over religion, all religious matters were therefore reserved to the exclusive authority of the states.

Anti-federalists, on the other hand, believed that powers already delegated by the Constitution might be exercised by the federal government in ways, as yet unspecified, that could restrict speech, establish and aid religion, and so forth, unless the use of these powers was curbed by explicit amendments.[12] The Federalists probably agreed to support such amendments in order to get the Constitution ratified. Madison, in any case, though opposed to a bill of rights in principle, honored his own commitment by introducing in the First Congress two separate amendments on religious freedom. Both were firmly rooted in the theory of religious pluralism that Madison had espoused in the *Federalist Papers*.

The first of his proposed amendments was this: "The civil rights of none shall be abridged on account of religious belief or worship, nor shall any national religion be established, nor shall the full and equal rights of conscience be in any manner, or in any pretext, infringed." The second read: "No State shall violate the equal rights of conscience." Several objections were raised immediately on the grounds that these provisions might injure religion. Madison's reply emphasized his double concern to prevent coercion and to encourage a multiplicity of sects. He said "he apprehended the meaning of the words to be, that Congress should not establish a religion, and enforce the legal observation of it by law, nor compel to worship God in any manner contrary to their conscience." He "believed that the people feared one sect might obtain a pre-eminence, or two combined together, and establish a religion to which they would compel others to conform."

After discussion and modification by two committees (Madison was a member of one), the amendments went to the full House. Samuel Livermore of New Hampshire moved the following: "Congress shall make no laws touching religion, or infringing the rights of conscience." This was again modified by a version proposed by Fisher Ames of Massachusetts, which the House finally adopted: "Congress shall make no law establishing religion, or to prevent the free exercise thereof, or to infringe the rights of conscience." The House also passed Madison's second amendment regarding the states. In the Senate this second amendment was immediately dropped, no doubt because of suspicion of federal power over the states, and the first House amendment was changed again: "Congress shall make no law establishing articles of faith or a mode of worship, or prohibiting the free exercise of religion." This revision was apparently not acceptable to the House, however. A conference committee of both houses, of which Madison was a member, then produced the final form that we have today: "Congress shall make no law respecting an establishment of religion, or prohibiting the free exercise thereof."[13]

The Riddle of the Establishment Clause 47

We shall never know whether Madison actually composed this final version, since the documentation is so incomplete. The main issue, in any case, has never been whether or not the words of the amendment were his, but rather what they meant precisely. Did they represent a single original intent or only an original consensus? A heated debate in recent years has come to focus on the establishment clause. Is this the governing clause, with religious freedom *defined* by the absolute character of the separation?[14] In other words, did the establishment clause intend to restrict Congress from passing any laws at all regarding religion (which seems to have been Madison's principle), or did it really intend to permit some form of government support for religion as long as this did not prefer one religion to another?[15] The latter alternative would mean that free exercise, not disestablishment, was the governing principle, that Congress was being charged primarily with the care of religious freedom, and that federal involvement in religious matters could be justified to the extent that it promoted such freedom.

Each side of this debate has been trying to find clues of exact intent through minute analyses of whatever records survive. In the end neither array of arguments is wholly convincing, and the controversy will very likely never be settled, simply because not enough evidence exists, and what does exist is ambiguous on many points. The truth probably lies somewhere between the two alternatives. That is to say, the establishment clause did not necessarily mean the same thing to all the framers. In regard to wording, for example, it is clear that it was not Madison but Ames and Livermore (both from states with establishments) who supplied the verbal core of both clauses. Madison said his most valuable proposal was the one prohibiting states from violating rights of conscience, but that proposal was rejected. Hence the clauses cannot be said to express his thought *tout court*.

On the other hand, the clauses clearly did not repudiate

his views entirely or he would certainly have objected publicly. We must remember that, like all the "enlightened," Madison believed everything could be settled by compromise. Because he wanted agreement on the form of the amendment, he very likely accepted phrasing he did not fully approve but finally could not change. On the Senate side the original wording indeed supports the position that the intent was no more than to prohibit the preference of one group to another. This version was not finally adopted, however, though the reasons for its rejection are unclear. Collectively, the majority of the Congress seems to have meant something more by *non-establishment* than simply the safeguarding of religious freedom. But how much more?

This is precisely the question we cannot answer with any degree of certitude, although we do have one action by this First Congress indicating that "more" did not signify the total non-involvement of the federal government with things religious. The same legislators who enacted the First Amendment also, with no dissent from Madison, readopted in 1789 the Northwest Ordinance of 1787, first passed by the Continental Congress, the third article of which read as follows: "Religion, morality and knowledge, being necessary to good government and the happiness of mankind, schools and the means of learning shall forever be encouraged." After citing this bit of evidence, Walter Berns pointedly remarks: "It is not easy to see how Congress, or a territorial government acting under the authority of Congress, could promote religious and moral education under a Constitution that...forbade all forms of assistance to religion."[16] Also, in the course of debating the First Amendment, the First Congress recommended a day of national thanksgiving and prayer. Encouragement of religion in general is evident, finally, in the fact that public taxes at the time were paying for military, legislative, and prison chaplains.

We must conclude, then, that we can know what the

framers meant by the religion clauses only up to a point and not beyond. All of them, whether for religious or for civic reasons, wanted the numerous religious bodies to flourish in society in complete freedom. All of them wanted to prohibit a *national* establishment of religion, while saying nothing about existing *state* establishments. All of them wanted to prohibit any intrusion by government into any individual's freedom of conscience, whether this freedom be of a specifically religious nature or not. This broad consensus on general policy, however, was driven by large differences in motivation. To use John Courtney Murray's distinction (though not in a way he would have approved), for some framers the two clauses were simply "articles of peace," good and prudent lawmaking made socially necessary by the "contagion of liberty"; for others they were just as surely "articles of faith," either theological convictions that freedom from government was a religious imperative or Enlightenment ideologies that such freedom was a natural right.[17]

While Madison "stood at the forward edge of Congress, pushing it clearly to require a greater degree of separation...than many members desired,"[18] his influence was neither exhaustive nor singular. The framers were certainly moved by his conviction that religious freedom should be limited neither by religious institutions nor by government and that all such institutions should be denied the support of government power. But we cannot determine the degree of this influence. Beyond this we have only guesswork. This guesswork is vastly compounded if we ask about the intentions and motivation of those many members of the state legislatures that eventually ratified the First Amendment, since records of these assemblies are as sparse as those of the First Congress. In the end, therefore, we have to acknowledge that too many minds and motives were at work; too many differences and ambiguities surfaced on secondary issues; too many compromises went into the vagueness and grand simplicity of the text.

Protestant Hegemony in the Nineteenth Century

While the framers of the First Amendment were creating a legal framework to protect religious freedom and to distance the federal government's power from religious institutions, the majority of Americans were already beginning to think of their new nation in explicitly religious terms. What was taking place in the law was disestablishment; what was taking place in the culture was fusion. The machinery and functioning of the federal government became officially secular; the attitudes of the people toward their government remained explicitly religious.

There is much irony here. The First Amendment guaranteed that there would be no intrusion by the national government into the nation's religious affairs. But these religious affairs were overwhelmingly Protestant in character, constituting an ethos which had flourished from earliest colonial times. The commitment to religious freedom meant that in the nineteenth century this Protestant ethos was to become what has been called a "de facto establishment," a Protestant cultural hegemony. This had enormous consequences for society in general and for government in particular, and it will repay us to examine these now. The American achievement of religious liberty did not take place in a vacuum but in a particular time and place and with specific historical and cultural consequences.

The first consequence of this Protestant hegemony was that the United States became, unofficially but in effect, a Christian nation. What Robert Handy refers to as "the long spell of Christendom" now began to take root in the culture. "The vast majority of Americans," writes Thomas Curry, "assumed that theirs was a Christian, i.e., Protestant country, and they automatically expected that government would uphold the commonly agreed on Protestant ethos and morality. In many instances they had not come to grips with the implications their belief in the powerlessness of government in religious matters held for a society in which the values, customs and forms of Protestant Christianity thoroughly permeated civil and political life."[19]

An even more authoritative witness of this social phenomenon is Joseph Story, a justice of the Supreme Court in the early nineteenth century. In his *Commentaries on the Constitution* Story wrote that "there will probably be found few persons in this, or any other Christian country, who would deliberately contend, that it was unreasonable, or unjust to foster and encourage the Christian religion generally, as a matter of sound policy, as well as of revealed truth." He also believed that "probably at the time of the adoption of the constitution...the general, if not the universal, sentiment in America was that Christianity ought to receive encouragement from the state."[20]

Christianity was thus thoroughly woven into the fabric of society in the 1800s and was easily accommodated to various forms of local establishments. In Massachusetts, for example, the state constitution endorsed both religious freedom and an official state Protestantism:

> As the happiness of a people, and the good order and preservation of civil government, essentially depend upon piety, religion, and morality: Therefore, to promote their happiness and to secure the good order and preservation of their government, the people of this commonwealth have a right to invest their legislature with power to authorize and require, the several towns, parishes, precincts, and other bodies politic, or religious societies, to make suitable provision, at their own expense for the institution of the public worship of GOD; and for the support and maintenance of public Protestant teachers of piety, religion and morality....[21]

What took place on the state level in Massachusetts had its replica on the more local levels also. There developed what William Lee Miller terms "a voluntary-coercive way of looking at society." The First Amendment had, as he put it, "deregulated the religion market," but the resulting free market was not neutral; it favored the evangelicals, the revivalists and the pietists who thrived on all those tactics of persuasion—revivals, missions, conversions— which government now encouraged. During this Second Great Awakening, as it is now called, "the religion of 'enthusiasm' flourished, and soaked the nation's culture in its characteristic themes."[22]

In this "pan-Protestant enterprise," however, there were different kinds of volunteering. The direct emotional appeals of the revivalists insisted on results, and in multiple ways people were compelled to act freely in matters religious. Miller's rich analysis links this particular kind of "voluntarism" with an eagerness to impose morality by resort to law. This "spirit of righteousness" eventually succeeded in enacting blue laws for Sabbath observance, liquor laws, and a large variety of other laws to promote the good society. The impulse toward religious liberty thus worked to provide institutions in society through which Protestantism could fulfill itself.

The prime example of this effort to impose a public good was the defense and penetration of the public schools. Robert Handy makes it clear that Protestantism's extraordinary support of this enterprise was based on the conviction that the public schools were to be a primary agent for making America Christian. They represented not a secularizing influence but a patriotic and civilizing influence, into which the Protestants who controlled them could inject the teachings, practices, and especially the morality of the mainline churches. "Protestants were generally agreed that the elementary schools need not be under the control of particular denominations, for their role was to prepare young Americans for participation in this broadly Christian Civilization toward which all evangelicals were working." The various states thus carried on at local levels a system of public education in which practically all the traditions and most of the influences were in fact religious. "Evangelical leaders saw no reason why the schools should

The Riddle of the Establishment Clause 53

not continue to be bearers of Christian civilization, unofficially, of course, but effectively." Hence any criticism of public schools "seemed to most Protestants to eat away at the foundations of the Christian America they envisioned."[23]

Protestant hegemony in the nineteenth century had a second consequence for society: a religious dimension came to be recognized as integral to the nation's political experience. Such a religious dimension had, of course, been present from the time the nation was founded. Franklin, Jefferson, and John Adams originally proposed that this new beginning be symbolized on the Great Seal of the United States by Moses crossing the Red Sea. "The basic reality of their life was the analogy with the children of Israel," writes Daniel Boorstin of the colonists. "They conceived that by going out into the wilderness they were reliving the story of the Exodus."[24] This conviction was made explicit by the Latin words at the top of the Great Seal, *annuit coeptis*, "He has favored our undertaking." Such a sense of divine destiny is certainly not peculiar to Americans; to some extent it is an ingredient in the self-consciousness of every people. What was peculiar was the interpretation Americans gave to this formative experience: they translated it into the experience of Israel's exodus from Egypt. In other words, they were not just a rebellious people; they were a chosen people with whom God had entered into a covenant and whose subsequent history was to be inextricably entwined with a faith experience.

This cross-fertilization of religion and politics at the start of the republic was doubly reinforced by the domination of Protestantism in the century following. The legal ties between religion and the national government may have been severed, but the cultural ties grew ever stronger, tightened by the religious conviction that God had destined America to play a special role in world history. Protestantism thus came to represent not simply religion in

America but "American religion." This religious dimension of national experience has been given various names by sociologists and historians: "civil religion," "public religion," "public theology," "societal religion," "the religion of the republic."[25] The common denominator of all these very differently nuanced titles, however, is agreement that the political had gradually become a dimension of the religious and the religious a dimension of the political. That is to say, national experiences, practices, and behavior came to be interpreted by both religious and civil authorities in the light of some transcendent reference.

The civic symbols that accompany this interpenetration (public rituals like presidential inaugurations, and celebrations like Thanksgiving Day, Memorial Day, and the Fourth of July) are really marginal to the phenomenon and should not distract us from the fact that we are dealing here with the more interior realm of motivational myths. A myth in this sense is that which declares our relationship to the world of reality; it preserves a concrete human experience, not by describing it so much as by transforming it, by giving insight into its meaning, so that it provides moral and spiritual motivation for individuals and society. As an empirical fact, the origin of the United States was the successful rebellion of thirteen colonies against England. But this event was immediately perceived as a special destiny under God, an "exodus" to a future in which America was chosen to demonstrate for all the world the possibilities for freedom and happiness in a constitutional republic.

The Civil War of the 1860s shattered this confidence, bringing home a recognition that this was also a land of oppression, that its people had responded to the call of God in a profoundly ambiguous way, and that at the heart of the American dream there was betrayal. Abraham Lincoln caught this disillusionment when he spoke of Americans as God's "almost chosen people."[26] The religious instincts that sparked the abolitionist movement before the

The Riddle of the Establishment Clause 55

war now brought public repentance during and immediately after. Lincoln's powerful images of sacrifice, death, and rebirth succeeded in purging the nation's guilt, and the Thirteenth and Fourteenth Amendments finally gave some legal dignity to blacks.

But this period of purgation was short-lived. Racial segregation gradually became institutionalized as the new form of oppression. The unchecked growth and independence of industrial capitalism raised moral dilemmas that religion scarcely recognized. The radical political individualism of American Protestantism (a product, as we saw, of pietist and enlightened perceptions of government as coercive) did not equip it to critique radical economic individualism. The robber barons and the captains of industry had such a free hand because there were no rules as yet in our Christian nation to check them. Nor were there any religious rules to judge the "manifest destiny" of the country's wars of expansion at the turn of the century. Indeed, as Sydney Ahlstrom emphasizes, it was precisely religious symbols that were used to sanction our aggression toward weaker neighbors. He writes:

> The churches reflected the American consensus—and then proceeded in the limited time available to convert the war into a crusade and to rationalize imperialism as a missionary obligation.... Kipling's words on "The White Man's Burden" became for a season the battle hymn of the republic. Never has patriotism, imperialism, and the religion of American Protestants stood in such fervent coalescence as during the McKinley-Roosevelt era.[27]

There was a third consequence of Protestant hegemony in the nineteenth century, both an extension of the second and a counterbalance to its extreme individualistic bias. This was the ideal of the good citizen. I have written elsewhere of the two very different traditions of good citizenship that came to the fore when the new nation was founded.[28] There was, first of all, the humane sociability of the Scottish Enlightenment, which most historians now agree was a major influence on Jefferson, Madison, and the other Founders. This tradition emphasized the moral requirements of citizenship thought to be essential for a republic in any recognizable relation to the republics of the Renaissance or ancient world. Central to these moral requirements was "public" virtue exercised through participation in self-government and disinterested concern for the common good. It is easy to see why these moral requirements of republicanism appealed so much to American Protestants. For them, as Robert Handy notes, morality was the all-important link between religion and civilization. "Protestants generally accepted the separation of church and state, but stoutly resisted any sense of the separation of religion and morals from public wellbeing... and felt that their contribution of a religiously based morality was especially important to the whole."[29]

Even though this republican "virtue" became crystalized as an ideal in the Declaration of Independence, it always remained open on the practical political level to combining in various degrees with another outlook on citizenship originating from a very different historical tradition. This second tradition, also present in our culture from the start, was driven by a utilitarianism that, in its pure laissez-faire liberal form, would say that the common good is what automatically emerges when each citizen pursues his or her own economic self-interest. John Locke is usually named as the source of this concern for property and marketplace. Such "commerce" had its own virtue for the artisans, shopkeepers, and petty bourgeoisie of the new nation: it brought them the capital that the republican landed gentry already possessed. Classic republicans, on the other hand, saw an exclusive concern for commerce as constituting "corruption," the very antithesis of public virtue, totally distracting the citizen from concern for the common good.

But such exclusive concern for "commerce" does not

seem to have been all that widespread. Apparently there were never very many adherents either of classic republicanism or classic liberalism; most Americans of the eighteenth and nineteenth centuries were a mix of both. This is certainly true of Madison and the others who framed the Constitution. The rhetoric of virtue they used in the Declaration of Independence and during the Revolution was genuine at the time and remained so afterward, but it became softer. When these statesmen came to compose a practical instrument to rule the country, they realistically tried to provide for institutions that could preserve liberty even when the majority of citizens lacked such public virtue. Checks, balances, and a separation of powers were thus all built into the new federal structure, because, as *Federalist Paper* No. 51 tells us, there had to be a "policy of supplying by opposite and rival interest, the defect of better motives."[30] This was also one of the reasons for the form of representation in the new Constitution. Elected officials were expected to be the true elites, the primary examples of public virtue, placing the common good above local good and mediating on the national level any conflicts of self-interest.

Following the enactment of the establishment clause, however, the federal government began distancing itself from any concern to educate the populace in moral matters. Socializing citizens into thinking morally and acting virtuously became the exclusive responsibility of the states (since these were unaffected by the establishment clause), and it was the churches that usually carried out this responsibility on the various local levels in these states. More often than not their instrument was the public school, whose civic and moral values they controlled. Sydney Ahlstrom gives one example of how this happened: the enormous influence in the nineteenth century of McGuffey's graded *Readers*. Before the century's end over 120 million copies, with their various stories, essays, and histories, had helped shape the American mind, forging "an ever closer bond between Protestant virtue, national ideals, and literary values."[31] This is what Alexis de Tocqueville actually saw taking place in the 1830s. Religion contributed to public life by inculcating personal standards of conduct without which a democratic society could not function. In his mind the moral restraint imposed by the churches was precisely what would channel the crass commercial self-interest of Americans into moral boundaries. "The main business of religions," he observed, "is to purify, control, and restrain that excessive and exclusive taste for well-being which men acquire in times of equality, but I think it would be a mistake for them to conquer it entirely or abolish it. They will never succeed in preventing men from loving wealth, but they may be able to induce them to use only honest means to enrich themselves."[32] He therefore called religion "the first of their political institutions," because it safeguarded the moral standards of the people, influencing their attitudes, behavior, and manners, and so made them better citizens.

Even though churches were multiple, de Tocqueville found this morality to be everywhere the same. He saw it working especially through family life, in the great respect Americans had for marriage. Giving the new nation a high degree of domestic stability, he said, inevitably contributed also to stability in the public sphere.[33] Michael Walzer has referred to such an outlook as a "pluralist concept of citizenship," a citizenship mediated through associations that act in the public interest, like church, family, school, and neighborhood. Sociologists now speak of these as the "soft structures" of society, dealing with human motivation, value generation, and value maintenance. "Citizenship (as a moral choice rather than as a legal status) is possible... only by joining other groups along with the state."[34] In the last century de Tocqueville already recognized the importance of such voluntary associations for nurturing good citizens and providing them with meanings and identity. "The morals and intelligence of a democratic people," he concluded, "would be in as much danger as its commerce and industry if ever a government wholly usurped the place of private associations. . . . Nothing, in my view, more deserves attention than the intellectual and moral associations in America."[35]

2. Revising the Founders' Legacy

Disestablishment Nationalized

These three consequences of Protestant cultural hegemony — the Christian character of the nation, the religious dimension of politics, and the ideal of the good citizen — constituted a very broad socializing process, educating people for civic responsibility in a republic seen as having a destiny under God. Religious and political values thus became inextricably connected in the public mind, even though the establishment clause of the First Amendment had severed all institutional bonds between the churches and the national government. This unusual historical situation was made possible precisely because, as we saw at the start, none of the original amendments to the Constitution had any application to the states; these assertions of freedom were limitations on the federal government only.

In the case of the religion clauses, this did not mean that the states were any less committed to religious freedom and the protection of religious conscience, something long achieved in the nation as a whole and almost never challenged. Nor did it mean that direct financial support of particular churches or their preferred treatment were ever seriously advocated on the state or local levels. Even though four states still had established churches when the First Amendment was enacted, these were all short-lived, because the wisdom of legally separating religious and civil institutions was soon generally recognized. What did happen as a result of this independence from federal jurisdiction was the sort of accommodation to religion by local government that existed in the nineteenth century, which we have just described. There was everywhere an official encouragement of ethical and spiritual beliefs, symbolized most strikingly perhaps by a strong church presence in public schools, but operative also through Sunday closing laws and the prohibition of gambling and alcohol. Until well into the twentieth century such local cultural meshings of the civil and the religious raised no legal problems at all in the context of the First Amendment.

During this whole period the federal government could involve itself in free exercise or establishment disputes only if these arose between two states or in territorial areas not yet states. In the 1880s and 1890s, for example, a federal polygamy statute was enforced against the religious convictions of Mormons in Utah and Idaho, but this was because these areas were still federal territories. Otherwise, no legal dispute on the state or local level could ever be brought into a federal court based on the religion clauses of the First Amendment. All this was to change, however. In order to see why and how this change took place, we have to go back to 1868, when the Fourteenth Amendment was enacted in the wake of the Civil War, to protect the rights of ex-slaves whose freedom had been secured under the Thirteenth Amendment. Section 1 contained three now famous clauses:

> No state shall make or enforce any law which shall abridge the privileges and immunities of citizens of the United States; nor shall any state deprive any person of life, liberty, or property, without due process of law; nor deny any person within its jurisdiction the equal protection of the law.

The second of these, the "due process" clause, is identical in wording with the "due process" clause of the Fifth Amendment, except that in the Fourteenth it is the states, not Congress or the federal government, that are enjoined against depriving any person of "life, liberty or property." On its face the phrase "due process" would seem to refer

The Riddle of the Establishment Clause 61

only to a procedural restraint on the power of state governments. Proper procedures, in other words, such as trial procedures in criminal cases, must be followed in order to secure a person's "procedural rights" to life, liberty, or property. (This had always been the understanding of the due process clause of the Fifth Amendment.) But very soon after the Fourteenth Amendment was enacted attempts were made to convert the understanding of the clause into a substantive restraint. That is to say, the argument was made that the general words "life, liberty or property" were meant to refer to and to absorb (or "incorporate") those very specific substantive prohibitions and guarantees contained in the Bill of Rights.

This claim, that the Fourteenth Amendment guaranteed "substantive due process" or "substantive rights" (in addition to procedural due process or procedural rights), was obviously aimed at limiting by the Bill of Rights those legislative goals that state governments had up to then legitimately pursued. In 1878 and again in 1884 the Supreme Court explicitly rejected this claim.[36] However, the justices did not hesitate over the years to "incorporate" or absorb into the due process clause other substantive rights which were not specified by the first eight amendments to the Constitution.

This process of incorporating other substantive rights into the Fourteenth Amendment began at the turn of the century. Laissez-faire economics, for example, dominated American business at the time, and eventually this ideology found its way into Supreme Court decisions that invalidated various state attempts to regulate the unfair treatment of employees. The owner of a business had certain "economic rights," said the Court in the most famous of these decisions, which must be regarded as "liberties" within the meaning of the Fourteenth Amendment and hence protected from state regulation.[37] Before 1925 the Court also identified many other substantive rights, none of which were mentioned in the Bill of Rights:

the right of the individual to contract, to engage in any of the common occupations of life, to acquire useful knowledge, to marry, establish a home and bring up children, to worship God according to the dictates of his own conscience, and generally to enjoy those privileges long recognized at common law as essential to the orderly pursuit of happiness by free men...."[38]

In 1925, however, in the landmark *Gitlow* case, the Supreme Court affirmed for the first time a relationship between the substantive rights or specific guarantees of the Bill of Rights and the due process clause of the Fourteenth Amendment. It thereby swept aside the denials of fifty years and began what one legal historian has called "a metamorphic constitutional process that has not yet been brought to a conclusion."[39] The Court said: "We may and do assume that freedom of speech and of the press — which are protected by the First Amendment from abridgement by Congress — are among the fundamental personal rights and 'liberties' protected by the Due Process Clause of the Fourteenth Amendment from impairment by the states."[40]

In 1937 the Court added to this list another First Amendment right: "The right of peaceable assembly is a right cognate to those of free speech and free press and is equally fundamental."[41]

Finally, in 1940, the Court took the major step of incorporating the religion clauses. It said in *Cantwell* v. *Connecticut*: "The fundamental concept of liberty embodied in [the Fourteenth] Amendment embraces the liberties guaranteed by the First Amendment. The First Amendment says that congress shall make no law respecting an establishment of religion or prohibiting the free exercise thereof. The Fourteenth Amendment has rendered the legislatures of the States as incompetent as Congress to enact such laws."[42] This absorption of the religion clauses into the Fourteenth Amendment illustrated the theory which the Supreme Court has followed since *Gitlow*: the

The Riddle of the Establishment Clause 63

most fundamental rights of persons are protected against state abridgement through the Fourteenth Amendment's due process clause, and some of these fundamental rights are to be found in the Bill of Rights. These are indeed so central that we cannot imagine any definition of liberty without them.[43]

Nonetheless, the justices have never accepted the thesis that the framers of the Fourteenth Amendment intended to make the entire Bill of Rights applicable to the states. Rather, they have opted for a process of "selective incorporation." This process has enabled the Court to bypass the extremely complex question of what Congress actually intended in 1868 in regard to the Bill of Rights. Scholars who have meticulously scrutinized identical historical data have reached diametrically opposite conclusions on this question, and their work has generally polarized the Supreme Court.[44] The most we can say with certainty today is that the precise legal extent of Section 1 of the Fourteenth Amendment was clearly not the chief focus of discussion for its framers and that to search for the meaning in their minds at that time is probably to seek from history more than history can provide.

Far more important for our purposes than this dubious original intent of Congress in 1868 is the fact that from 1940 on the Supreme Court began to use the Fourteenth Amendment to apply to the states both religion clauses of the First Amendment. The Court's rationale for this application raised few problems in the area of free exercise, since it was not at all difficult to see how religious liberty could be regarded as a fundamental right to be protected by substantive due process. The neuralgic issue, as we shall see in a moment, was how precisely this rationale could justify applying the establishment limitation to state and local communities. Yet the application itself had momentous consequences for religion, both for good and ill. In any event, the establishment clause now became "nationalized," applicable not simply to the federal government but to every state and local government as well.

What this entailed was the elimination of all regional diversity in dealing with the precise mode of separating religion and government, at least in principle. Disputes previously settled in state and local courts, in accordance with regional laws and customs, were now governed by constitutional law and could be brought into federal courts. When combined with the expansion of federal government power in the twentieth century, this nationalization was clearly a moving of the earth under the traditional legal and religious landscapes. Litigation dealing with government vis-à-vis religion mushroomed in federal courts. A fundamental transformation began to take place in regard to how religious groups and interests should be treated. The relationships between government and religion, culturally stabilized for over a century and a half, were never to be the same.

Two fundamental and residual problems emerged from this nationalization of the establishment clause. One was historical and the other analytical. Both problems appeared in the famous *Everson* v. *Board of Education* case of 1947 and were carried forward in its wake, the one modified and mitigated, the other remaining acute. The importance of *Everson* is that it was the first case to use the establishment clause to judge a specific action by a state government.[45] The issue was the busing of students to parochial schools. A New Jersey statute, aimed at protecting children from traffic dangers, authorized bus transportation for all children and reimbursement to parents for money spent in such transportation. Justice Hugo Black, writing for a five-to-four majority, stated that the establishment clause forbade government to fund religious education, while the free exercise clause prevented it from denying public welfare benefits to Catholics who sent their children to parochial schools. Busing, however, was neither a funding problem nor a discrimination problem; it

The Riddle of the Establishment Clause 65

fell into a third category of "permissible" public welfare benefits. New Jersey could, therefore, but did not have to, provide safe transportation for all school children.

This landmark case raised, as I said, a key historical problem connected with the nationalization of the establishment clause. In the course of his opinion Justice Black opted for a very rigid theory of separation: the meaning of the establishment clause, he said, is that government can do absolutely nothing, by its programs, policies or laws, to aid or support religion or religious activities. This theory he traced back to the views of Jefferson and Madison, which he understood to have been enacted into the First Amendment. But, as we saw earlier, there is only ambiguous historical evidence to support the belief that the First Congress meant exactly what Madison and Jefferson meant by disestablishment, and evidence of what the ratifying states may have meant is even less clear. As far as we know, there was no single original intent of the framers, only an original consensus among them. The "wall of separation" metaphor, which Jefferson casually coined in an 1802 letter and which Black claimed to be normative, would certainly never have been accepted by the majority of those who enacted the religion clauses.

Just prior to the *Everson* case the Court had offered two much narrower understandings of disestablishment. In the 1940 *Cantwell* case (which first applied the establishment clause to the states), the establishment prohibition had been interpreted as an assurance of religious liberty, that is to say, of freedom from coercive laws that could compel unwilling persons to participate in religious ceremonies. And in 1943 the Court tried to suggest an even narrower interpretation, namely that disestablishment, as nationalized, could be reduced to a guarantee of free speech (and so the nonparticipation for religious reasons of a Jehovah's Witness in a flag salute was really an exercise of freedom of expression that could not be limited by the states).[46] Such narrow interpretations of disestablishment would hardly have prevented states and local communities from continuing to favor religion in various ways. Once Black adopted the much broader Jeffersonian concept in *Everson*, however, any favoring at all of religion became an issue of the greatest importance; now disestablishment would prohibit not merely those practices that infringed liberties, but any state action whatsoever which aided one religion or all religions.

In the long line of cases that constitute *Everson's* progeny, the justices as a group have never repudiated either its no-aid theory or its historical justification. Yet the historical problem it raised has been modified, because in practice the absolute character of no-aid and its historical warrant has been softened. The *Everson* decision itself offered some grounds for this: the justices who held for strict separation also developed the doctrine of "indirect aid" to religion through "permissible" public welfare benefits (such as busing children to parochial schools). In subsequent cases over the last forty years, the justices have been much more attracted to Madison's benign metaphor of a movable "line of separation" rather than to Jefferson's impregnable "wall" metaphor, very likely because they wanted to avoid charges of hostility or indifference to religion. As a result there has gradually developed over the years a concept of "benevolent neutrality," allowing a zone of voluntary accommodation and legislative discretion—a kind of "play in the joints" between the two clauses. The Court has thus continued to support paid chaplains for legislatures and the armed services, exemption of religious income from taxation, and the legal observance of religious holidays; and it has approved such practices as the availability of school facilities for meetings of student religious clubs and tax allowances for fees paid either to public or parochial schools.[47]

In practice, therefore, disestablishment today means a prohibition against sponsorship and interference, but it also means the avoidance of government entanglement through pragmatic maneuvering between the permissible promotion of religious freedom and the impermissible promotion of religious belief. In other words, the degree of government participation in the sanctioning and support of religious practices must be balanced with the corresponding impact of these practices upon freedom of belief and conscience. We shall have occasion later to deal at greater length with this concept of accommodation. For the present it is sufficient to note that the historical problem connected with *Everson* has far less significance today than it had in 1947.

The importance of religious freedom in many establishment cases, however, highlights the second problem connected with nationalization, a problem not of history but of legal analysis. The Court's theory has been that the fundamental freedoms of the First Amendment have been absorbed into the phrasing of the due process clause of the Fourteenth Amendment because this clause protects the fundamental rights of persons against state abridgement. But, as we have seen, Justice Black's position in *Everson* was that the establishment limitation means the prohibition not merely of liberty-infringing establishments but of all government action that would aid one religion or all religions. How precisely such aids, when they do *not* deprive persons of liberty or property, can be brought within the Fourteenth Amendment (and so applied to state and local communities), Black did not bother to explain. He seemed to assume that the 1940 *Cantwell* case, which first asserted the absorption of both religion clauses, had determined the question (though, as we also saw, Black gave a much broader interpretation to disestablishment than did *Cantwell*). The question then arises of how a state or local government can deprive someone of liberty or property without due process simply by infringing the establishment clause, in the meaning given to it by the *Everson* decision?

Two Justices have tried, unsuccessfully, to answer this

question. Justice Felix Frankfurter suggested in a concurring opinion that the separation of religion and government had become a nationally accepted principle when the Fourteenth Amendment was adopted in 1868 and is therefore today one of those institutions fundamental to our conception of liberty.[48] But if this were the case, would it not follow that the concrete ways that government related to religion in the nineteenth century should really become the norm for its present meaning in American life? This logical conclusion is probably the reason that the Court as a whole has never embraced Frankfurter's explanation. Justice Brennan proposed in another concurring opinion that, because the establishment clause co-guarantees one's religious liberty along with the free exercise clause, freedom from state involvement in religious affairs could well be thought of as a fundamental right.[49] But, one might object, given the wording of the Fourteenth Amendment, should it not rather follow that a violation of the establishment limitation would raise a due process question only if it had the effect of restricting personal or property rights — such as coercing one's conscience or forcing one to pay taxes in support of government-sanctioned religion?

It is therefore no easy matter to explain how infringing the establishment clause, as *Everson* understood it, can deprive someone of liberty. Would this difficulty not suggest some tempering of the establishment limitation in the course of its application to the states? In contrast to its impact on the federal government, the limitation against the states might well be understood as effective only insofar as it is, in a given case, "essential to the scheme of ordered liberty."[50] Yet the Court as a whole has made use of none of these due process considerations, whether substantive or procedural, either to explain how precisely the establishment clause applies to the states or to temper its application. Over the years it has remained relatively unconcerned that some state legislation regarding religion which does not affect liberty (or affects it only remotely) may be judged nonetheless to constitute a privation of liberty without due process of law.

How, then, has the Court explained this incorporation of the establishment clause and its application to the states? In a 1963 case dealing with a Pennsylvania statute requiring daily Bible reading in the public schools, Justice Tom Clark said that he need give no explanation, since the holdings of previous cases provided sufficient precedent (though none of these had answered the question either). In fact his 1963 opinion sought to minimize the coercive aspects of the Pennsylvania law, insisting that an establishment clause violation (unlike a free exercise violation) need not be predicated at all on the assurance of religious liberty. Because of these previous holdings, he said, the whole dispute now had significance as an academic exercise only.[51]

Yet the consequences of pursuing such an "exercise" could well have been startling. One might have found, for example, that there is no justification for treating state governments as strictly under the Fourteenth Amendment as the federal government must be treated under the First Amendment. One might even have found that states, unlike Congress, could actually aid religion insofar as they did not affect the religious or other constitutional rights of individuals and could be restricted in such aid only insofar as they thereby unreasonably violated these rights.[52] Nor must we suppose that such a development (i.e., nationalizing only those establishment restrictions that affected personal rights of religious liberty) would have meant that issues such as school prayer, Sunday closing laws, or state aid to religious schools could not have been litigated. As these caused difficulties in any given locality they could all still have been legally contested, but not in federal courts. Such controversies would have been limited to state and local judicial decision, and the inevitable changes in society that resulted would have been achieved on a state-by-state basis.

Prayer in public schools is the perennial example. In areas where almost everyone is a member of the same religious denomination, the issue of what prayers to say and whether to say them would probably not arise at all (unless local practice could be shown to coerce someone's religious freedom). On the other hand, in areas of the country that were thoroughly pluralistic religiously, local court challenges to prayer in public schools would undoubtedly have had the same result as present Supreme Court decisions. This will be seen more easily if one takes into account the fact that, between 1877 and 1913, thirty-three states amended their constitutions to prohibit financial aid to church-operated schools. Hence allowing leeway to the states in the establishment area would hardly involve widespread risk of excessive entanglement between religion and state governments. Nor should it be forgotten that the equal protection clause of the Fourteenth Amendment now sets clear limits to state power, limits which did not exist when the First Amendment was adopted, and may not even have been envisioned when the Fourteenth itself was written. The dangers, therefore, of leaving a certain discretion in establishment policies to states would certainly not be great and would probably put far less strain on the national social fabric as well as on the federal system generally.[53]

One voice on the Supreme Court has called attention to this legal analysis problem that we have been considering. Justice William Rehnquist said in 1976 that, in his opinion, "not all of the strictures which the First Amendment imposes on Congress are carried over against the states by the Fourteenth Amendment."[54] The Court as a whole, however, has shown little inclination thus far to reexamine the paucity of its legal reasoning on the precise weight to be given to the nationalization of the establishment clause. As of now, consequently, "settled law" places exactly the same legislative restraints on state and local governments regarding establishment as it does on the United States Congress.

But will this law continue to be "settled"? Former Chief Justice Warren Burger once said that the purpose of the religion clauses "was to state an objective, not to write a statute."[55] The Court therefore faces the continuous task of developing principles and policies that realize the objective without freezing the clauses at any particular time into a rigid cultural mode. Constant reinterpretation by local statutes will certainly be necessary, along with new applications of these statutes in the light of new social, political, and religious developments. As we shall see presently, it was such cultural change that gave rise to nationalization in the first place, and future cultural change could well be a catalyst toward a new consideration of the meaning of the religion clauses.

A Second Disestablishment

We have been scrutinizing the radical change that took place in the interpretation of the establishment clause as soon as that clause became applicable to all state and local governments through absorption into the due process clause of the Fourteenth Amendment. I want to avoid the impression, however, that the sole source of this change was a judicial rethinking of constitutional law. By far the more potent source was the cultural breakdown of the Protestant hegemony that we described earlier. Robert Handy has termed this breakdown, which took place roughly during the years between the two world wars, our "second disestablishment," and it is important for us now to know in some detail why and how it happened.

The "first disestablishment" of religion by the Founders was exclusively legal. Its social effect, as we saw, was negligible, both because of the dominance of Protestantism and because of the limited reach and applicability of the First Amendment itself. The "second disestablishment" of religion, however, was not legal at all but, rather, sociological. It nevertheless accelerated the legal process of the amendment's nationalization, because it was Protestantism's ethos that had in a sense held the religion clauses in escrow for over a century and a half. As William Lee Miller puts it, the decline of this ethos finally brought these clauses "out of the vault" to impact society with their own vast potential for cultural change.

This "second disestablishment" began with the immigrants who came in successive waves just before and after the turn of the century, most of whom were either Catholics or Jews. Before the mid-1900s both these groups had consolidated themselves into very articulate social and political minorities, the strength of the Catholic minority manifesting itself finally in the 1960 presidential election of John F. Kennedy. During this same period Jewish communities had likewise begun to assume public status of equality with Catholic and Protestant churches. Religious pluralism eventually came to be taken for granted even more than ethnic diversity. The hyphenated adjective "Judaeo-Christian," unknown in America before the twentieth century, became in the course of the 1940s and 1950s the symbol of shared moral values and tradition.

Will Herberg's well-known sociological study of the period, *Protestant-Catholic-Jew*, highlighted this generally accepted tripartite division, though it did not, even at that time, adequately describe either the true diversity of the pluralism or the large number of unchurched whose secular faiths laid equal claim to American loyalty. The great merit of Herberg's book was that it identified a "consensus Americanism," a "common religion," which was at mid-century both increasingly religious and pervasively secular.[56] How would such a new configuration react to the vestiges of a de facto Protestant establishment, which had by then been in place for well over a hundred years?

Added to this pervasive religious pluralism and growing secularism was another important sociological development: the expansion of government activity (some would say intrusion) into almost every aspect of American life. The "welfare state" (insofar as this exists in the United States) is the most obvious example of this, because here the legislative use of spending, taxation, and regulatory authority is so highly visible. (Few people are unaffected by Social Security and unemployment insurance.) But the same expansion has taken place in education. Even if largely operated by the states, compulsory public schooling is now usually federally supported and funded, involving government in the daily lives of almost everyone. The Supreme Court's continuing use of the Fourteenth Amendment to extend federal limitations on state action reflects this expanding nationalism and declining localism in our public life.

Generally Americans have had no great problem with this increased government involvement on the community level. Indeed it has been welcomed by many, especially by churches aware that they are no longer able to meet the educational and welfare needs of their members. But this expansion of the federal government inevitably involved it directly in matters religious as well. When this happened there was always danger that government might either impinge upon religious liberty (thereby violating the free exercise clause), or give its support, financial or otherwise, to certain religious practices (thereby violating the establishment clause). Bible reading and prayer in public schools became the most blatant examples of the second danger, because they had the highest potential for government endorsement. But the first danger was perceived as equally threatening, and sensitivity to its risk accounted for the Court's spirited defense of freedom of conscience when faced with such state restrictions as Sunday closing laws and sabbath employment practices.

These dangers of government involvement were aggravated by the fact that religious pluralism had become so widespread on the national level, even though it may not always have been reflected on the local scene. Catholics and Jews were beginning to wonder why their children in public schools had to participate in essentially Protestant religious exercises. Sabbatarians wanted to know why they had to obey Sunday laws. Mormons objected to government restrictions on their efforts to implement fully their religious beliefs through rules of conduct. The common element in all these instances was an experience of coercion. The remedy for this experience, however, was much more complex and elusive when its source was the subtle vestiges of Protestant establishment than when its source was some government restriction of religious conscience.

The Supreme Court was not overly sensitive at first to this new religious pluralism, and, as we saw, it waited a long time before extending to the states and other localities all those establishment restrictions that originally bound only Congress. Had not these structures of spiritual commitment, many asked, been in place on the local level for over a century and a half? Indeed they had been. Were not the state and local authorities entitled, then, to safeguard them by imposing some modest restrictions on the liberty of those who explicitly renounced them? For a long time the Court had no answer to this question. When it finally did act in the establishment area, beginning with the 1947 *Everson* case, its decision, as we saw, was to develop and enforce a *national* policy. That is to say, it did not simply reappraise certain religious practices of a particular state, sanctioned by a long history of Protestant cultural domination.

That the Court reacted precisely in this way to religious pluralism (and to subtle coercions like Bible reading and prayer in public schools) can be explained to some extent by the whole thrust of its Fourteenth Amendment jurisprudence, which was clearly national in character: expanding federal activity simply did not favor localism in public life. But this would explain only the reach of Court decisions, not the substantive content of that reach. Moreover, as we also saw, beginning in 1963 the Court ceased to require proof of any coercion of religious freedom in order to find violations of the establishment clause. Hence the coercion issue could not have been of itself the determining factor in the Court's reaction to religious pluralism. Some other value operative in American society had to be guiding the Court, at least initially, in formulating this interpretation of the First Amendment.

There is good reason to believe today that this other value was equality. To understand why this concept could have such a decisive influence on the Court's initial approach to religious pluralism we have to recognize the transformation of the American consciousness that took place between the late 1940s and the late 1960s by which equality became a major object of government policy. Inequalities of class, race, religion, and sex, which previously had been accepted almost as part of the natural order of things, gradually came to be seen as deeply colored by injustice and exploitation. *Brown* v. *Board of Education*, which declared segregation unconstitutional, surely acted as one catalyst for this new level of popular awareness. But another was the sudden realization that widespread poverty still existed in the midst of general national affluence. Concern for inequalities sharpened this sensitivity, both because poverty was one of their direct results, and because mass demonstrations of the period dramatized the economic plight of large segments of our minority populations.

As a result of such awareness and concern the federal government not only made laws but constituted itself the instrument of egalitarian policy. Courts, in their turn, were forced to scrutinize a variety of legislative and executive choices demanded by these egalitarian pressures. The judgment of one historian of this period is that "when the standpoint from which the Supreme Court was obliged to view the requirements of equal protection . . . and when the principles of fairness which even the more conservative judges now regarded as constitutionally normal, are compared with those of an earlier generation, the difference to be observed amounts to a far greater transformation both in the distribution of opportunity and the obligations of government than in any period that has occurred since the American Revolution."[57]

Despite often bitter disagreements as to methods and aims, a nationalization of consciousness thus emerged at this time which had no precedent in American history. Such a unified national interest in regard to a specific moral principle is an extremely rare phenomenon in American life; the decentralized and morally pluralistic principles of federalism have always been regarded as the most unity attainable or even desirable in national politics. Yet in 1987 a striking confirmation of this continuing national concern for equality appeared in a *New York Times*/CBS News Poll on the success of the Constitution: over 50 percent of the respondents said they thought the Constitution was doing a poor job of treating all people equally.[58]

"When the constitutional history of the central decades of this century comes to be written," said Harvard's Mark de Wolfe Howe in 1965, "I feel quite sure that the key to understanding its turbulence will be the concept of equality."[59] It is not indeed very difficult to see how this concept might galvanize the Supreme Court's defense of religious freedom, because such freedom, like the long-smoldering problems of racial discrimination, was an issue that involved clear moral principle and universal human right.[60] However, unlike racial equality, religious freedom was long since achieved in principle, never tore apart the nation's moral conscience as did segregation, and only now and then presented the Court with challenges from individuals or sects regarding alleged infringements on such freedom.

The Riddle of the Establishment Clause 77

While in theory, therefore, the concept of equality was focused on the protection of religious conscience, in practice little was really being challenged in our society that needed such protection. The focus thus naturally shifted to establishment issues, because there was an obvious logical connection between the legal consequence of religious pluralism (that all sects are equal before the law) and the establishment principle (that between these sects the government must maintain a discrete neutrality). If any government were to give public support to one sect only, we could scarcely claim that there prevailed either equality among denominations or government neutrality in matters religious. One might even say, as one legal scholar has, that this logical connection works "to make the rule of neutrality and the rule of equality in this area essentially one."[61]

But the logic of this connection pushed the Court, in the early years of establishment litigation, to a conclusion that went far beyond dismantling the vestiges of Protestant cultural hegemony or insisting upon the equality of all religions before the law. In its genuine concern to make equality the central objective of constitutional government, the Court began to find in the establishment clause not only a barrier against laws favoring one religion or all religions; it also found, in these same assurances with respect to religion, matching assurances with respect to irreligion. In other words, the principle of equality was used not only to safeguard belief, but also to protect unbelief.

This was clearly the thrust of Justice Black's rule in *Everson* that the First Amendment "requires the state to be a neutral in its relations with groups of religious believers and non-believers."[62] Black made this point again in dissenting in a 1952 case: "The First Amendment has lost much if the religious follower and the atheist are no longer to be judicially regarded as entitled to equal justice under law."[63] This broadened rule of neutrality, by which religious and irreligious interests are seen as equal, clearly follows from Black's rigid and absolutist approach to separation. But it follows even more clearly from the court's preoccupation during this time with the concept of equality.

Now the problem here is not the protection of unbelief. Even the Founders were convinced that what they called "infidelity" should be respected. The skepticism of the Enlightenment was far too pervasive for them to think of the new nation in terms of religion triumphing over irreligion, however significant religion might have been at the time for the majority of Americans. Indeed, before the Bill of Rights was added in 1791, the Constitution's only reference to religion was to prohibit it as a test for holding public office. Hence in spite of the wishes of evangelical America, in the nineteenth century as well as today, there has never been nor is there now any legal question of denigrating the citizen status of the atheist or the agnostic.

But, in the minds of the Founders, was it the establishment clause that protected this status? Does it make constitutional sense to remove this clause from its historical context, where it spoke only of religion, and make it speak of irreligion? If there were no other constitutional means at hand giving unbelievers the same security provided for believers, then, of course, such reliance on the establishment clause might well be justified. But, as Mark de Wolfe Howe has observed:

> The facts of text and history tell us... that the First Amendment's assurance of freedom of speech and press is wholly adequate to meet the need and the desire for security for doubting minds and denying words. When that initial assurance was later supplemented by the Fourteenth Amendment's provisions with respect to equality and liberty — religious and irreligious — the occasion for distorting the manifest objectives of the religion clauses of the First Amendment had been removed.[64]

It has been argued that such an observation is purely

The Riddle of the Establishment Clause 79

"academic," since the Supreme Court actually did choose to use the establishment clause to protect the right of unbelievers not to be touched in their civic capacity by anything religious.[65] But this ignores the point of Howe's comment, namely that the Court's extension into the establishment area of the national impulse toward equality has necessarily had a negative influence on the role of religion in society as a whole, something the justices as a group clearly never intended. For this stance of the Court does not in fact tend to enforce neutrality, but rather tends in principle to give nonreligion the edge over religion in what is essentially a conflict not over equality but over culture. This is what the late Justice Potter Stewart was getting at in his dissenting opinion in the 1963 *Schempp* case (which struck down prayer and Bible reading in public schools): "refusal to permit religious exercises thus is seen, not as the realization of state neutrality, but rather as the establishment of a religion of secularism, or at least, as government support of the beliefs of those who think that religious exercises should be conducted only in private."[66]

Stewart was wrong to conclude that *Schempp* or other cases dealing with prayer, Bible reading, and other religious practices in public schools were badly decided — a sufficient element of social and psychological coercion was present in these vestiges of Protestant hegemony to justify the judicial outcomes. Nevertheless, the fact remains that a preoccupation with equality led the Court early on to speak about its neutrality in ways that went beyond underlining the secular character of government, both federal and state. By the mid 1960s the Court seemed to many in the nation to be insisting upon a secular character for American *society*. It seemed to be ferreting out religious influences in public life and to be fostering the impression that religion was irrelevant to the public good. There was no element of coercion, for example, in the famous *McCollum* case of 1948, which outlawed voluntary released-time programs on public school premises for instruction by various religious groups. Yet with Justice Black's opinion in this case the Court began to speak of these schools as if they were, and ought to be, symbols of our nation's secular unity and indispensible instruments for mediating that unity. In this same case Justice Frankfurter's problem with released-time programs was precisely their divisiveness, their tendency to separate children into groups of Catholics, Jews, Protestants, and unbelievers.[67]

The justices were well aware that their decisions during this period were being interpreted as manifestations not of neutrality toward religion, but of hostility or at least indifference. Those who cared about this public image felt compelled in various opinions to give assurances to the contrary. Justice Douglas said in 1952 that "we find no constitutional requirement which makes it necessary for government to be hostile to religion and to throw its weight against efforts to widen the effective scope of religious influence."[68] Even Justice Black was anxious that a 1962 decision should not seem to some "to indicate hostility toward religion or toward prayer. Nothing, of course, could be more wrong."[69] Justice Brennan's concurring opinion in the *Schempp* case a year later emphasized that "forms of accommodation will reveal that the First Amendment commands not official hostility toward religion, but only a strict neutrality in matters of religion."[70]

It was these "forms of accommodation" that eventually allowed the Court to develop, in the course of many decisions of the 1970s and 1980s, its theory of "benevolent neutrality" (which has, as we have seen, gone far to soften much of its earlier language of absolute separation).[71] Tax exemption for churches, for example, was meant to "accommodate" religion, said Chief Justice Burger in 1970.[72] And in 1983 he could defend the opening of legislative sessions with a prayer by saying that the practice "has become a part of the fabric of our society."[73] Prayer in public schools and financial assistance to parochial schools remain the only large establishment areas today where the strict separation language of *Everson* still commands majority support. The reason may well be a tacit agreement, by a very large segment of society, that if an absolute separation can be maintained here, then the ideal of separation will be secure, and accommodation may be more easily tolerated elsewhere, in order that our other ideal of benevolence toward religion may also be secure.

In any case, what remains at present is a fairly well articulated and stable nationalized policy, as opposed to the former understanding of disestablishment that allowed for different policies in different states and local communities. We must not forget, however, that this situation represents a true transformation in the relationship between government and religion in America, one that can be traced to the extraordinary religious pluralism of our day as well as to this century's preoccupation with the concept of equality. What is quite clear also is that the original intentions of the framers of the First and Fourteenth Amendments, while always the starting point for the Court's decisions, have had relatively little to do directly either with the timing or the content of this transformation.

Nor has this second disestablishment turned out badly for America. The problems we face in the religious area today stem not so much from our having removed the vestiges of Protestant hegemony as from our not yet having replaced this once dominant religious culture with one corresponding to the new religious pluralism of our secularized society. There is surely no lack of effort on the part of religious people to articulate such new interdependencies of government and religion, but the obstacles to this enterprise are formidable. It will repay us now to look at some of these obstacles more closely, for the enterprise itself may be suggesting some legal and social developments

A Third Disestablishment

I have been underlining the extent to which Supreme Court decisions in the establishment area have resulted from constitutional law interacting with religious pluralism and the drive for equality. While both these phenomena continue unabated today, a third phenomenon has appeared in recent years and will undoubtedly characterize the second half of our twentieth century: a widespread breakdown of any common agreement on key matters of personal and public morality. Such moral pluralism has so far been much more disruptive for the nation than religious pluralism. The latter dislodged Protestantism as our culture's religion, but it left intact the commonly accepted and biblically based value system of the "Judaeo-Christian" tradition.

Gradually, however, this value system began to have less and less success in adapting to the growing secularization of American society. By the late 1960s and 1970s the youth counterculture had exposed the many tensions and contradictions in the old religious value system, and in the 1980s the resultant moral pluralism began being referred to as a "third disestablishment" of religion.[74] Like the "second disestablishment," this "third disestablishment" was a social not a legal phenomenon, but, as we shall see, it will very likely affect future Supreme Court decisions regarding religion's role in our society. This will become clear as we examine the phenomenon more closely and consider its current legal impact.

Moral pluralism found its catalyst in America when secularization combined with religious pluralism. It is important to recognize that "secularization" is a sociological term and does not of itself have any pejorative connotations for religion. In its most general sense it refers to that "process by which sectors of society and culture are removed from the domination of religious institutions,"[75] a process that began in the West well before the colonies became a nation and that secured its legal synonym in America through disestablishment. More specifically it is "the process by which religiously-legitimated states are transformed into secularly-legitimated states."[76] In this narrower sense secularization refers less to changes in beliefs or behavior than to the legal relationships between religion and government. As we have already seen, this movement said nothing about the erosion of religious influence or the demise of religious institutions in the new nation, nor does it today. It says simply that the power relationships between religion and government have shifted and that their dominant roles may no longer be compatible.

This historical and generally healthy stress upon the autonomy of human values, often referred to also as "secularity," has to be sharply distinguished from an ideology which absolutizes the human to the exclusion of all openness to a transcendent sacred reality. "Secularism" is the usual name given to this ideology, which is hostile to all claims of the sacred and seeks to exclude religious influence from the life of society. While this distinction is a real one, in practice there is sometimes a very fine line between an action that promotes the latter and one that simply recognizes the former. This became very apparent, for example, in the *Schempp* case discussed above, when Justice Stewart accused the Court of propagating a "religion of secularism," while the other justices were obviously convinced that they were doing nothing of the sort.[77]

This catalytic impulse toward moral pluralism, I must repeat, has not entailed any lessening in the vigor and vitality of religion in America. From a sociological point of view it has simply meant that now the various religious value systems have to compete under conditions of a voluntary "market." In spite of this relatively benign effect on religion as such, secularization has nevertheless produced great anxiety in many religious people because they see their Judaeo-Christian tradition apparently unable of itself any longer to provide a commonly accepted public and private morality. Without such basic moral consensus, they ask, can our nation long survive?

This anxiety has fostered numerous efforts by mainline churches to dialogue with the nonreligious segment of society in an effort to find consensus on at least some basic issues of common social life. Participants in such dialogue generally acknowledge that a certain degree of moral pluralism may be more or less permanent in the private sphere and that this means not total disagreement on what is good but rather a self-limiting consensus. Moral pluralism, in other words, is not moral chaos. "We need as many different moral concepts as we do," says Jeffrey Stout, "because there are so many different linguistic threads woven into the fabric of practices and institutions as rich as ours."[78]

Not all these linguistic threads are functioning equally well, however, and this has put serious strain on the current public dialogue. The research of Robert Bellah and his collaborators indicates that the current moral vocabulary of many persons is one dominated by personal self-fulfillment and financial success and that our biblical and republican traditions have been receding into the background, their public languages eroded by the expressive and instrumental individualism that has become our primary language today.[79] An emphasis on individual consciousness and on discovering one's inner self has apparently had a deep effect on American religion, moving expressive individualism from the fringes of religious communities to a place at their center. "Almost imperceptively," says one sociological study, "this notion of religious voluntarism, long affirmed in principle for religious collectivities, has been extended to individuals as well. This new voluntarism is now part of the culture; it will take on features as yet unknown but it will not go away."[80]

In such an atmosphere moral rules are inevitably judged by fluid standards, a diversity of styles, and changing common beliefs. This tends naturally to homogenize moral language and to foreclose public conversation and disagreement on issues that continue to perplex persons and the nation. Despite this privatization of faith, however, data indicate that renunciation of religious identity is relatively rare. The secularity of religious individualists somehow paradoxically combines with loyalty to religious institutions, producing people who have been characterized as "religio-secular" and "bilingual."[81] But because such an outlook involves a growing subjectivism in belief and practice, the result is that moral pluralism has now become internal to those very institutions most traditionally responsible for human motivation and moral guidance, not only churches, but schools, families, and neighborhood and ethnic groups as well.

These institutions now appear much weaker in their capacity to transmit ethical standards, because individuals determined to stand and fall on their own do not need these mediating institutions to protect their values, however much they may need them to satisfy their inner psychological needs. Nor is this to say that the social values espoused by such institutions are unimportant for the common good; ecology, peace, and feminism, for example, are hardly insignificant public issues. The problem is that these values are usually detached from the political order, with weak social organization, and so tend to encourage that contemporary impulse of government to intervene directly in local affairs in order to nationalize procedures and standardize moral practice.

The impact of this third disestablishment upon the current legal interface between religion and government will immediately be evident when we consider the challenge of the religious New Right. For if moral pluralism has threatened to erode the coherence of that Judaeo-Christian tradition that once unified Americans, the dogmatic fundamentalist crusade against it now threatens to overwhelm all moderating influences, whether religious or secular. I am reminded of the words of an anonymous seventeenth-century writer once quoted by Robert McAfee Brown: "I would rather see coming toward me a whole regiment with drawn swords than one lone Calvinist convinced that he is doing the will of God." John Steinbeck's preacher Casey sees the same thing in *The Grapes of Wrath*: "One person, with their minds made up, can shove a lot of folks around."

The formidable political front that fundamentalism has mounted against what it sees as threats to traditional Protestant and American values has come as a total surprise to many, especially the secularists, who had managed to ignore for most of the twentieth century this very large body of traditional Christian believers. These fundamentalists have now identified certain social conditions as intolerable, and they have the resources to mobilize for change in these conditions. In his well-documented study of the movement George Marsden explains that these fundamentalists are evangelicals in that revivalist tradition that dominated America for a large part of the nineteenth century. What set fundamentalism apart was its alarm over the early theological and cultural trends of this century and its sponsorship of a militant crusade against what was then called "modernism" and is now called "secular humanism."

Like all revivalists, fundamentalists believe in the absolute inerrancy of the Bible, the necessity of a conversion experience, and the importance of a holy life. Beginning in the 1950s the Moral Majority developed from this heritage and soon began to focus on "secular humanism" as a quasireligious force threatening to displace Christianity entirely from the culture. Always alarmed at any moral decline they might perceive, fundamentalists now devel-

The Riddle of the Establishment Clause 87

oped a conspiracy theory which found "secular humanism" to be responsible not only for the moral pluralism in the country, but also for all recent decisions of the Supreme Court on religious questions.[82] Their response to moral ambiguity was to draw the sharpest distinction between good and evil, one that polarized moral attitudes between satanic relativism and multiple stringent absolutes. This dualistic revival continues unabated today, not only in its extreme form but also in more modest guises that appeal to large segments of middle America. The reason for this appeal is that most mainline religious people, while by disposition not militant at all, still believe that the Judaeo-Christian value system ought somehow to be privileged in this country.

Because there exists in the nation as a whole a longing for the moral certainties of the past, the majority of Americans are still looking for constants, beliefs they can rely on in the midst of accelerating change. Religion still makes a difference in their lives, and their fears are immediately aroused when they hear it has been displaced by "secularism." Why, they ask, should "secularism" become privileged in this country? If there is to be a disestablishment of religion, why should there be an establishment of irreligion? Why should the nonbeliever, whose freedom has been guaranteed by believers, suddenly become dominant, able coercively to exclude religion from the public sphere?

This general concern for moral values in the country received sharp focus from fundamentalists in 1987 through three legal challenges. All three dealt with religion in public schools, an unsurprising fact since, as we saw, public schools are as close as we have come as a nation to a religious establishment. Two of these three challenges concerned elementary and secondary school textbooks. In Greenville, Tennessee, seven fundamentalist families initially won the right in Federal District Court to withdraw their children from reading classes and pro-

88 *The Riddle of the Establishment Clause*

vide them with alternative instruction because they found that the Holt, Rhinehart and Winston basic reading series could cause a child to "adopt the view of a feminist, a humanist, a pacifist, an anti-Christian, a vegetarian, or an advocate of a 'one-world' government" — all concepts contrary to their religious beliefs. The Sixth Circuit Court of Appeals overruled the decision, saying there was no evidence that students, in reading such books, were required to affirm or deny a religious belief or to do anything against their religion. Had the parents been able to prove such coercion, the outcome would undoubtedly have been different.[83]

The second textbook challenge took place in Mobile, Alabama, where a federal judge was presented with the challenge that "secular humanism" was being promoted in Alabama schools. He agreed with the plaintiffs that this is a form of religion "for First Amendment purposes," because it had been designated as such by the Supreme Court. (The Court did this almost parenthetically in a footnote to a 1961 free exercise opinion that broadened the meaning of "religion."[84]) He also agreed that this "religion" was being established by thirty-nine textbooks in history and social studies, all of which unconstitutionally ignored the role of Christianity and Judaism in America and so had to be removed from Alabama's public schools. As expected, the decision was reversed by the Eleventh Circuit Court of Appeals, which saw immediately that designating "secular humanism" as a religion was simply a springboard for the fundamentalists' legal challenge. But did the texts in question actually promote the beliefs the challengers said they promoted? The Appeals Court said simply that the purpose behind the thirty-nine texts was clearly not religious, a judgment which surprised no one, since publishers are well aware that promoting an ideology does not sell books. The Court indicated, moreover, that the First Amendment requirement that govern-

The Riddle of the Establishment Clause

ment be neutral toward religion could not be turned "into an affirmative obligation to speak about religion."[85]

In each of these two cases law was being used as a last resort to remedy what for the plaintiffs was an intolerable situation, one in which public school texts no longer spoke of their religion or their moral values. A third test of this legal remedy, one that finally reached the Supreme Court in 1987, was the "creation science" controversy. This arose in an effort to protect the literal accuracy of the creation story in Genesis, long felt to be one of the true "fundamentals" of Christianity. The defenders of literal accuracy hold that Genesis tells us not only who made the universe but precisely how it was made. The discovery of evolution and its eventual appearance in science courses in public schools thus posed an immense threat, because it amassed scientific evidence for a very different "how." In the minds of the fundamentalists evolutionary theory also implied, though scientifically it could never actually say, that there had been no initial "creation" at all.

Early in this century laws were passed in many states prohibiting the teaching of evolution outright. All of these were eventually struck down by the Supreme Court.[86] The fundamentalists then shifted to an equal-time strategy. But for this to work the Genesis story had to appear to be taught, not as a religious alternative to evolution, but as a scientific alternative. While the fundamentalists were primarily concerned with advancing scientific evidence that attacked evolutionary data, they also constructed tortuous arguments aimed at compressing all events of the earth's history into the few thousand years of biblical chronology, and at showing that all fossils are products of a great flood. Because science teachers as a group generally refused to teach these materials as part of their courses, equal time for "creation science" had to be secured through state laws, two of which were eventually passed in 1981 in Arkansas and Louisiana.[87]

Before dealing with these two state laws we should note

that opposition to biological science does not mean that all fundamentalists are necessarily anti-intellectual. George Marsden insists that learning for them reflects a genuine intellectual tradition going back to the Puritans, but one that is alien to most modern academics. "Their attacks on evolutionism reflect their awareness that the developmentalist, historicist, and cultural assumptions of modern thought have undermined the certainties of knowledge." They are thus much more attracted to the pre-Darwinian philosophical assumption that an objective look at "facts" will bring a higher yield of truth.

It is no accident, for example, that many leaders of the creation science movement have degrees in applied science and engineering, and so tend to view the Bible as a collection of true and precise propositions. Henry Morris, the principal architect of creation science theory, has a Ph.D. in hydraulics. He began, he says, with the statements of Genesis and then, "being an engineer, I looked for solid evidence." This compatibility of fundamentalist thought with the technological strand of modern culture explains much of fundamentalism's appeal today.[88] A 1983 Gallup poll came as a great surprise to many because it found that 44 percent of Americans agreed that "God created man pretty much in his present form at one time within the last 10,000 years."[89]

The Arkansas and Louisiana cases illustrate this intellectual appeal of fundamentalism. Both states passed laws requiring that public school teachers give "balanced treatment" to creation science and evolution; if one was taught, the other also had to be taught. In 1982 a federal judge in Little Rock found that the purpose of creation science was clearly religious, and that the Arkansas law violated the establishment clause because the motivation of the legislators was to promote a religious belief.[90] Arkansas did not appeal this decision, but Louisiana did eventually appeal to the Supreme Court when its Creation Act was declared unconstitutional for the same reasons.

Writing in 1987 for a seven-to-two majority, Justice Brennan concluded that "the pre-eminent purpose of the Louisiana Legislature was clearly to advance the religious viewpoint that a supernatural being created humankind." He dismissed as a "sham" the legislature's contention that its aim was to foster academic freedom for competing scientific theories on human origins. The act, he said, "actually serves to diminish academic freedom by removing the flexibility to teach evolution without also teaching creation science." A long dissent by Justice Antonin Scalia, joined by Chief Justice Rehnquist, focused on the "scientific data supporting the theory that the physical universe and life within it appeared suddenly," which they believed was the basis for saying that the legislators had a secular purpose. The law should therefore be upheld, they said, unless further proceedings in a lower court found it unconstitutional on other grounds.[91]

These legal challenges of the fundamentalists serve to throw into sharp relief the contemporary tension in America resulting from the widespread indifference to many religious belief systems. Seeking to neutralize Darwinism by requiring public schools to teach fundamentalist doctrine disguised as science may well appear to be a misguided, benighted maneuver, legally doomed from the start. It is nonetheless symptomatic of the larger problem: the moral pluralism of our third disestablishment threatens the cherished values of large numbers of religious Americans, who now experience the social and religious orders as deeply fragmented. Their strongly held views of society, though perhaps not as extreme as those of the fundamentalists, are not going to go away because of some Supreme Court ruling.

The earlier and more benign religious pluralism was somehow able to maintain a balance between these extremes of secular indifference and reactionary sectarianism, between moral incoherence and the rigidity of righteousness. Today these polarities are pulling farther apart. The center is no longer holding. Those who expected religion to be a restraining influence are discovering that it can also release Dionysian passions. The aphorism of Martin Marty is increasingly apt: highly civil people are not very committed; highly religious people are not very civil. Tribal claims of the various religious bodies are meshing less and less with the unitive claims of the broader national culture. The American experiment with religious diversity thus continues to reveal its perennial tensions and ambiguities, as well as the rich texture of our national religious psyche.

From one point of view the Supreme Court ought not be involved at all in this cultural crisis. It is not the Court's function to take sides on institutional disagreements between believers and unbelievers. Such religious tensions are not like racial tensions. In the area of the establishment clause we are not dealing with matters of universal human rights, which strike deep chords in the public conscience and cry out for judicial protection. "Can one imagine," asks William Lee Miller, "sending federal marshals to smash a crèche on a public common, or break up eighth grade prayer groups in the gym?"[92] From another point of view, however, the Court is obliged to settle the legal controversies that come before it, because some actions of public officials may not in fact be permissible under the religion clauses. The question, therefore, is not whether the Court should intervene in a strictly cultural crisis, but how precisely and to what extent it should intervene. Thus far we have been charting the course of this intervention in our past and present. We must now ask about the future.

3. Reconsideration and Compromise

Accommodation as Catalyst

The social phenomena we have been examining under the two rubrics of "second disestablishment" and "third disestablishment" inevitably raise the question of the nature of American society. The Founders, as we saw, clearly wanted a federal government unconnected institutionally with any particular religion, but they just as clearly recognized the religious character of their society and, whether for religious or secular purposes, they all wanted religion to flourish among the people. That is why, in the nineteenth century, when our religious culture was essentially Protestant, state and local governments freely supported religious aspirations and practice. Alexis de Tocqueville wrote in 1835 that "America is still the place where the Christian religion has kept the greatest real power over men's souls."[93] Almost a century later, an English visitor saw little change. America, he wrote, is "a nation with the soul of a church."[94]

In 1892 Justice David Brewer could state categorically in a Supreme Court opinion that "this is a Christian nation,"[95] to be echoed by Justice George Sutherland in 1931: "We are a Christian people, according to one another the equal right of religious freedom, and acknowledging with reverence the duty of obedience to the will of God."[96] In 1952 Justice Douglas, faced with the obvious religious pluralism of our mid-century, quite properly changed the focus in his famous dictum: "We are a religious people whose institutions presuppose a Supreme Being."[97] The second part of his statement has been criticized as simply untrue historically, though I think it is also basically correct, insofar as the majority of citizens have always believed that religious ideas permeated our colonial origins and that religious significance somehow attached itself to our institutions.

These observations of Brewer, Sutherland, and Douglas were all true enough at the time, from a historical and sociological point of view, but they cannot be taken as statements of principle. The secular undertakings of most Americans may continue even today to have strong religious underpinnings. But our institutions of government and law, though formally acknowledging the existence and sovereignty of God, can only be secular, with essentially secular purposes, namely the maintenance of public order, justice, peace, and freedom. There is nothing specifically religious, much less Christian, about any of these purposes, carried out as they are today in a nation both religiously and morally pluralist.

This pluralism necessarily entails a continuous struggling together of religious and secular groups, a continuous interplay of opinion regarding both our common good and our public morality. But such pluralism also serves to moderate the resulting tensions and, more often than not, to urge reconsideration and compromise. I believe that there are two problem areas in the interrelationship of religion and government where in the future a willingness for compromise is especially desirable. In the first area such willingness will be required on the part of certain religious groups, and in the second area it will be required of the Supreme Court.

Many religious people have in recent years focused their concerns more and more on the issue of a religious presence in public schools. Their mistake has not been to have these concerns but to insist by their focus that these schools do what the rest of society has chosen freely not to do, namely to promote common convictions about religious truth and common agreements about moral action. The symbols of this insistence have been prayer and Bible reading in the classroom. It is now time for certain religious groups to recognize that compromises have to be made in both these areas. In regard to prayer, for example, it is at present the law of the land that "in this country it is no part of the business of government to compose

The Riddle of the Establishment Clause 95

official prayers for any group of the American people to recite as a part of a religious program carried on by government."[98] Justice Black was clearly correct in this 1962 opinion: government, in the guise of public school officials, simply has no competence in this area, however general or inoffensive the wording of any particular classroom prayer may be.

But this does not mean that it is not possible to have prayer in public schools. Outside the classroom any official student group may use school facilities to conduct worship services.[99] Inside the classroom it is possible for state or local governments to enact "minute of silence" statutes. The Supreme Court had indicated that offering students such opportunities for voluntary silent prayer would not violate the establishment clause. "The legislative intent to return prayer to public schools," said Justice Stevens in 1985, "is, of course, quite different from merely protecting every student's right to engage in voluntary prayer during an appropriate moment of silence during the school day."[100] Hence religious freedom can still be sufficiently accommodated without the enactment of state laws explicitly promoting prayer in the classroom.

Where reconsideration and compromise are most needed, however, is in dealing with religion as an appropriate subject matter of secular education. Religious people have simply not thought enough about the ways in which public schools can contribute to religious literacy without in the process becoming sectarian. The key question is how precisely to go about studying religious belief, as well as a sacred text such as the Bible. The Supreme Court has stated explicitly that such study itself is appropriate to public education at all levels. It has limited only the devotional use of the Bible, not its pedagogical use. "Nothing we have said here," insisted Justice Clark in the 1963 *Schempp* case, "indicates that... study of the Bible or of religion, when presented objectively as part of a secular program of education, may not be effected consistently with the First Amendment." Indeed, he added, "it might well be said that one's education is not complete without a study of comparative religion or of the history of religion and its relationship to the advancement of civilization."[101]

Justice Lewis Powell made the same point at greater length in 1987 in his concurring opinion in the "creation science" case:

> As a matter of history, school children can and should properly be informed of all aspects of this Nation's religious heritage. I would see no constitutional problem if school children were taught the nature of the Founding Fathers' religious beliefs and how these beliefs affected the attitude of the time and the structure of our government.... In fact, since religion permeates our history, a familiarity with the nature of religious beliefs is necessary to understand many historical as well as contemporary events.... The Establishment Clause is properly understood to prohibit the use of the Bible only when the purpose of the use is to advance a particular religious belief.[102]

This distinction between teaching the truth of a particular religious belief and teaching *about* it is crucial. It provides the legal key whereby the Judaeo-Christian tradition, and any other religious tradition, can enter into public school curricula. In the one case religion tends to be divisive; in the other case it is truly educative. Ironically, the chief difficulty in securing this second objective has been the power and influence of our religious pluralism: we have such a diversity of beliefs in America, with their competing claims and variety of tradition, that a certain tacit agreement has developed to avoid instigating controversy by not introducing any of these into public school curricula. Publishers have not been slow to draw the obvious corollary, and the result has been an alarming paucity of texts on secular subjects that deal adequately with religious themes.

An important report issued in 1987 by the Association for Supervision and Curriculum Development harshly

The Riddle of the Establishment Clause   97

criticized this paucity and suggested guidelines for including matters of religion in the curriculum. It stated flatly:

> Given the significance of religion and religious movements in the political and cultural history of the world, their virtual absence from today's social studies and history textbooks is particularly reprehensible.... Apparently, some people equate any treatment of religion in history texts with advocacy of specific religious ideas and publishers therefore avoid it.... Only when educators and parents demand critical instruction about the role of religion in world culture will such passages reappear in reading, literature, science, social studies, and history books.[103]

The report goes on to say that many of the assumptions that undergird present policies on religion in the curriculum are "incorrect, contradictory, or illogical." It notes with regret that students today would never know from their textbooks that religious groups were a vital force in the abolitionist and temperance movements of the nineteenth century or in the civil rights movement of the twentieth, or that world history and culture were critically influenced by religious thought. It nevertheless recognizes that separating the teaching *of* beliefs from teaching *about* beliefs often means walking a razor's edge. The dilemma will therefore continue to be how to keep both text and teacher neutral on the actual content of belief. That content, while properly the domain of church and home, can nonetheless be the occasion in school for exploration and discussion of moral issues, permitting a student to give expression to ethical insights from his or her own faith.

Those trying to do such teaching "about" religion on the elementary and secondary level should keep in mind the relatively secure status of religion courses in public-supported colleges. In part this is true because the Supreme Court sees education at this level as well as the courses themselves to be voluntary and not mandated by law.

College students are also more mature and less susceptible to indoctrination, and the potential of divisiveness is significantly less.[104] But this simply means that courses in religion on lower levels need to be very carefully structured. Teachers may be legally prohibited from arguing the case for Judaeo-Christian belief and morality, but it does not follow that concern for children's knowledge of America's religious tradition need be doomed to legal frustration.

What does have to be compromised in this development, then, is any attempt to indoctrinate. Educators and parents may well aspire to create in our elementary and secondary schools some intellectual integration between our predominantly secular public sphere and those religious values still prized by the majority of our citizens. These citizens, in other words, ought not expect to find public school curricula indifferent to religion. But in our present pluralist and progressively more secular society, public schools must inevitably perform a more limited function than they did in the past with respect to inculcating ultimate values. Better and less controversial forums exist to accomplish this laudable goal, namely the family, neighborhood organizations, church and synagogue. In these forums, moreover, there would be no coercion, but a manifestation of that voluntary tradition of persuasion which is at the heart of the First Amendment.

The type of compromise we have been considering from the point of view of certain religious groups is possible also on the part of the Supreme Court. For there exists in the Court's establishment jurisprudence a concept we have touched upon briefly already, that of "accommodation." This concept has never been adequately defined by the Court and is still in search of a theory, but the Court has nevertheless used it often. Chief Justice Burger said that accommodation was the result of "play in the points" between the two clauses. Legal scholars have now begun talking about it as a "zone" between them and are asking how wide this zone should be. Eventually the Supreme Court will have to answer this question. But as it does so, it will very likely be forced to reconsider some of its past decisions, thereby adding new elements to the riddle. These elements may indeed work toward the riddle's solution, but they may also simply add to its complexity.

The existence of a "zone" of accommodation was recognized as early as 1952, when Justice Douglas said in the *Zorach* case that when government "encourages religious instruction or cooperates with religious authorities...it follows the best of our traditions. For it then respects the religious nature of our people and accommodates the public service to their spiritual needs."[105] Douglas was explaining why releasing children for religious instruction away from public school property fell within an area of permissible accommodation, where government regulations may be adjusted to the religious needs of citizens. Otherwise, he said, government would be placed in a position not of neutrality toward religion but of hostility, something clearly at odds with the intention of the Founders. Such allowable government deference we might also call "voluntary" or "discretionary" accommodation, to distinguish it from an accommodation so obviously necessary that it would be mandated by the free exercise clause.[106] This voluntary character of the accommodation in question here is precisely what distinguishes it from sponsorship, since the latter by its nature always involves some element of government coercion. In the *Zorach* case there was neither coercion nor sponsorship, because public school grounds were not used for religious instruction, nor were students in any way required to attend religious instruction.

This distinction between promotion and accommodation lay more or less dormant for almost twenty years after *Zorach*, during which time the Court elaborated what has come to be called the *Lemon* test: for a government practice to be found neutral (and so constitutionally permissible), it must be clear that neither its purpose nor its direct and immediate effect is to promote religion, nor must it involve excessive government entanglement with religious bodies.[107] This three-pronged *Lemon* test has proved to be useful to the Court up to a point, but of itself it begs the question of whether what is at stake in a given case is indeed promotion or only an accommodation. Without this distinction virtually any government action that seeks to recognize the fact that "we are a religious people" could in principle be construed as having a purpose and effect that violates the establishment clause, thereby placing religion at a permanent disadvantage in society, something clearly not envisioned by the Founders. This did not in fact happen, because the concept of accommodation began to appear once again in Court decisions beginning in 1970.

The wave of litigation following the First Amendment's nationalization, combined with increased federal involvement in society, gradually created conflicts between the two religion clauses which had not previously existed. "The Court has struggled to find a neutral course between the two clauses," acknowledged Chief Justice Burger (who was the author of the *Lemon* opinion), "both of which are cast in absolute terms, and either of which, if expanded to a logical extreme, would tend to clash with the other."[108] In other words, as the Court found more and more things religious to disestablish, there developed greater and greater insistence on free exercise as a defense. Outlawed establishments began to reappear in the guise of preferred liberties. Hence the dilemma: if government is prohibited from favoring one religion over another, would not deference to such liberties (creating an exemption for one believer, while requiring all others to obey the law), effectively prefer the religion of one person over the religions of others? Would the Court not then be establishing the free exerciser?

Conflicts between the two clauses came to a head in 1970 in the landmark *Walz* case, in which the accommodation doctrine received its first extended articulation. The Court was asked whether the traditional property tax exemption for churches was not a promotion and establishment of religion. No, said Chief Justice Burger, the purpose of tax exemption was "not sponsorship, since the government does not transfer part of its revenue to churches." It was an effort to "accommodate" religion, by including churches "within a broad class of property owned by non-profit, quasi-public corporations." Such accommodation was a kind of "benevolent neutrality," allowing for "room for play in the joints," neither interfering with religion in a way forbidden by the free exercise clause, nor sponsoring it in violation of the establishment clause.[109] To emphasize this last point, Burger pointedly stated that, unlike the mandatory compliance imposed by courts when government is found to violate religious freedom, the voluntary compliance involved in permissible accommodation could not be reduced to a defense of free exercise. It rather existed in a zone between the two clauses, acting in this middle ground as a buffer against conflicts and as a force for harmony.

We might ask at this point, how wide should this zone of accommodation be? I want to suggest that it ought to be as wide as possible, and that for this to happen reconsideration and compromise will have to characterize the Court's future approach to disestablishment. While there is obvious need to keep religion and government legally separate, no "perfect absolute separation is really possible," because "we can only dimly perceive the lines of demarcation in this extraordinarily sensitive area of constitutional law."[110] Chief Justice Burger made these statements in 1970 and 1971 and echoed them in his 1983 ruling in favor of paid legislative chaplains: "The opening of sessions of legislative and other deliberative public bodies with prayer... has become part of the fabric of our society" and is "simply a tolerable acknowledgement of beliefs widely held among the people of this country."[111] In 1984

Burger once again spoke for the majority of the Court: "Nor does the Constitution require complete separation of church and state; it affirmatively mandates accommodation, not merely tolerance, of all religions." However, "no fixed *per se* rule can be found," added Burger. While the Court has often found the *Lemon* test helpful, "we have repeatedly emphasized our unwillingness to be confined to any single test or criterion in this sensitive area."[112]

In recent years the Court has in fact frequently supplemented the *Lemon* test with the accommodation approach, in order to resolve conflicts by seeking a middle ground between the demands of the two clauses. In 1981, for example, when the University of Missouri at Kansas City refused to allow religious groups to use space for worship, the case was brought to the Court under the establishment clause. But Justice Powell, writing for a majority of eight, focused his opinion rather on the free exercise and equal access rights of the religious groups. Having created a forum open to religious groups, he said, the University could not exclude a content-based exercise of religious speech. From the establishment side, he added, such an open forum situation does not of itself confer any state approval of religious practices.[113] Two years later, in 1983, a Court majority held constitutional a twenty-eight-year-old Minnesota statute that allows taxpayers to deduct from their state income tax the expense of tuition, textbooks, and transportation of dependents, whether these attend public or private schools. Justice Rehnquist said this did not constitute a support of religion (even though 90 percent of the taxpayers involved sent their children to religious schools), because it "neutrally provides state assistance to a broad spectrum of citizens." He then concluded:

> The Establishment Clause of course extends beyond prohibition of a state church or payment of state funds to one or more churches. We do not think, however, that its prohibition ex-

tends to . . . the sort of attenuated financial benefit, ultimately controlled by the private choices of individual parents, that eventually flows to parochial schools from the neutrally available tax benefit at issue in this case.[114]

When the type of voluntary accommodation allowed here to Minnesota is denied, however, because the Court applies the *Lemon* test too rigidly, there can be some odd results. This happened in 1985 when a five-to-four majority said that instruction by full-time public school teachers of secular subjects on parochial school premises was unconstitutional. The source of the problem was Title I of the Elementary and Secondary Education Act of 1965, which provides for remedial instruction of impoverished children. In New York City about 200,000 poor children were involved in this program, 22,000 of whom were in parochial schools. The city had originally required the parochial pupils to travel to public school buildings, but experience showed this to be too difficult. So the city decided to do what almost all Title I programs nationwide were doing, namely to send teachers into parochial schools during regular class hours. Periodically supervisors spot-checked to insure that instructors stayed clear of religious issues, thereby insuring that the clearly secular purpose of the program did not involve any effect that might seem to be promoting religion.

Justice Brennan, who wrote for the majority, acknowledged that this arrangement satisfied the first two *Lemon* tests, but he said that the supervision that was involved constituted "excessive entanglement" of government and so violated the third *Lemon* test. Justice Rehnquist called this approach a "Catch-22": aid must be supervised to insure no entanglement but supervision itself is held to cause such entanglement. The result was that, after twenty years without the slightest civic unrest, the line of separation now had to be drawn at the parochial school door. Officials around the country are now permitted to teach impoverished children in mobile trailers on the sidewalk outside, or on closed circuit television inside, or in nearby parks' or libraries (all of which some cities are actually doing), but they themselves cannot enter the building. This bizarre situation is based, as Justice Sandra O'Connor noted in her dissent, "on the untenable theory that public school teachers... are likely to start teaching religion merely because they have walked across the threshold of a parochial school."[115]

How far will the Court be willing to go in the future to accommodate religion? Much will depend on how rigidly the three-pronged *Lemon* test is understood and applied. The question will always be one of approximation and degree. To what extent is an exclusively religious purpose clearly evident in a given legislative act? How does one measure precisely whether and to what extent some effect promotes religion? At what point does a particular entanglement of religion with government become so significant as to make it unconstitutional? Also, once it is clear that accommodation is at issue and not crass sponsorship, how meaningful is it to ask whether the accommodation in question has a secular purpose or whether its effect is to encourage or advance religion? Do not all accommodations do this to some extent, including those mandated by the free exercise clause? "There are always risks," acknowledged Chief Justice Burger in 1971, "in treating criteria discussed by the Court from time to time as 'tests' in any limiting sense of that term. Constitutional adjudication does not lend itself to the absolutes of the physical sciences or mathematics. The standards should, rather, be viewed as guidelines with which to identify instances in which the objectives of the Religion Clauses have been impaired."[116]

The Ellipsis of Interpretation

One important conclusion can be drawn from the examination we have made of the establishment clause: its interpretation is destined to remain a riddle, a question forever puzzling, a problem always to be solved anew. This is because certain "ellipses" persist in spite of all efforts to interpret. Just as the omission of some element from a train of thought or speech produces puzzlement until that element is supplied, so certain elements seem to be permanently missing from our understanding of disestablishment. Interpretation constantly seeks to fill these gaps, both in order to ease our puzzlement and to deal effectively with cases pressing to be litigated. But the gaps remain. We have already examined three of them at length: the linguistic ellipsis between what the framers wrote and what they intended; the legal ellipsis between the nationalization of disestablishment and the concept of liberty in the Fourteenth Amendment; the sociological ellipsis between the Court's approach to separation and the popular conviction that such separation must not foster in society either indifference or hostility to religion. The persistence of these ellipses is a constant challenge to legal scholars, but thus far they have been unable to supply the missing elements to everyone's satisfaction. I think that there are three reasons why this will continue to be the case.

First of all, what we are interpreting is not static. To speak of the separation of government and religion is to address two realities constantly interacting with each other, whose respective roles in society are constantly changing. As the functions of government gradually expanded in our century, for example, its boundaries in relation to religion had to shift. The more that government intervened in local affairs, the more religion felt the impact. Following the nationalization of the religion clauses in the 1940s, any official support of a religious activity risked violating the establishment clause, while any government action that impinged on religious liberty risked violating the free exercise clause. Throughout the nineteenth century, by contrast, when government had far less influence on American life, the religion clauses had correspondingly less significance in constitutional law.

Hence we may well apply to the Constitution what Michael Walzer says of political documents in general: interpretation is not so much a controversy about a text but about ourselves; it is the meaning of our way of life that is usually at issue.[117] At certain historical moments that way of life may go through significant social, economic, or religious change. If such change should become concretized in a legal conflict that reaches the Supreme Court, the Court may have to ask whether the case before it demands a reinterpretation of some provision of constitutional law. In other words, the Court may have to find new ways to interpret its own legal tradition in order to facilitate the birth of new societal understandings and practice.

Paul Ricoeur has well described this interpreting process:

> The sense of a text, is not *behind* the text, but in front of it. It is not something hidden but disclosed. What has to be understood is not the initial situation of discourse but what points toward a possible world.... Understanding is not directed toward an author who is to be resuscitated. It does not even address his situation.... Understanding the text is to follow its movement from the sense to its reference, from what it says to that about which it talks. Beyond my situation as reader, beyond the author's situation, I offer myself to the possible modes of being-in-the-world which the text opens up and discovers for me.[118]

The Court fortunately has the great advantage of dealing with a document much of whose linguistic texture is open-ended enough to expand or contract in meaning. Its principles are cast in grand phrases, like "the majestic generalities of the Bill of Rights" (as Justice Robert Jackson once called them), or the Fourteenth Amendment's stern order to enforce "due process" and "equal protection." One of these grand phrases is the injunction that Congress

The Riddle of the Establishment Clause 107

"regulate Commerce with foreign Nations, and among the several States." During the nineteenth century this commerce clause was used to foster a free national market and mass production, but today the federal government uses it in the very opposite way, to restrain excesses in the market. The reason is that our economy came to be seen as a seamless web, and for the commerce power to be effective in our time, Congress had to be able to control those sources of production like agriculture, mining, and industry. In 1937 the Supreme Court reluctantly recognized this assertive view of the clause,[119] and Congress now acts as umpire of the national market, insuring that the rules are fair and that business follows them. This development is generally recognized as one of the most important constitutional events of our century.

Like the commerce clause, the establishment clause also cannot be understood from its origins alone. It is part of a living tradition that changes as the nation changes. In *Federalist Paper* No. 14 Madison noted that Americans "have not suffered a blind veneration for antiquity, for custom, or for names, to overrule the suggestions of their own good sense, the knowledge of their own situation, and the lessons of their own experience." This observation has surely been true of the Constitution. It is a document that has expanded its meaning in response to the expanding life of the nation, and nothing has been more part of that life than religion. "Our Constitution is not a straitjacket," wrote Justice Louis Brandeis. "It is a living organism. As such it is capable of growth — of expansion and of adaptation to new conditions.... Because our Constitution possesses the capacity of adaptation, it has endured as the fundamental law of an ever-developing people."[120]

There is a second reason that the establishment clause will continue to remain a riddle: no matter how much the relationship of religion and government may alter sociologically, the legal significance of the relationship at any given time is what the Court says it is. This gives to the justices extraordinary power to involve themselves in the culture of the country, since the controversies that come before them inevitably reflect the anxieties and ideals of society. This situation is complicated, of course, by the fact that membership on the Court does not remain the same, and so the judgment of one group of justices on a certain case may differ significantly from what the judgment of another group would have been. Nevertheless, at any given historical time they have to decide the degree to which they are going to rely on the Constitution to constrain the powers of the other two branches of government.

Legal scholars and political scientists are continually trying to explain how this power of the Court is consistent with the role of non-elected judges in our political system.[121] In the most controversial national issues, they say, our system makes it difficult, if not impossible, for either the legislative or executive branches to break a political stalemate; the Court alone is able to do so, thereby moving the country as a whole in a certain direction. Obviously this direction may be good or bad. In the history of racial conflict, for example, we see now that the direction of the *Dred Scott* decision (which declared blacks to be noncitizens and unprotected by the Constitution) was clearly bad, as was *Plessy* v. *Ferguson* (which legalized separate but equal treatment for blacks after the Civil War). But the direction of the *Brown* case (which finally outlawed segregation in 1954) was just as clearly good, creating as it did the impetus for the civil rights legislation of the 1960s.

Whenever cases arise with broad social implications, therefore, the inevitable question is always this: to what extent has the Court, in applying the Constitution to one or other case, been faithful to the original intent of the framers? In the vast majority of situations, said the late Alexander Bickel, the proper answer to this question is no answer. Seeking in historical materials relevant to the framers, or in the language of the Constitution itself, specific answers to specific present problems is to ask the wrong question. It may well be true, for example, that those who wrote the Fourteenth Amendment did not specifically intend to outlaw segregation, or to make applicable to the states all restrictions on the federal government stipulated under the Bill of Rights, but they did not foreclose such policies either and may indeed have invited them. This is because neither the framers of the Constitution nor the framers of the many amendments wanted what they wrote to be a catalogue of answers to specific questions to be asked sometime in the future. The Constitution was meant to be a charter of government, with chapter readings rather than complete text, very general principles usually, to be applied as need arose — by the legislative and executive branches first of all, but ultimately by the Supreme Court.[122]

In the *Brown* decision of 1954, for example, perhaps the most important Court case of the century, the justices concluded that "we cannot turn the clock back to 1868." In deciding the meaning of the Fourteenth Amendment, they relied not on the subjective views of the authors, but on the more general moral vision those views were seeking to serve. They had good reason to do this, for, as C. Vann Woodward has shown, racial discrimination and segregation of an extra-legal sort was widespread throughout the North in the late 1960s, with little legal effort made to remove it. Indeed, segregation as a system had been born in the North long before the Civil War and grew there contemporaneously with slavery in the South. "Racial discrimination in political and civil rights was the rule in the free states and any relaxation the exception." Immediately after the war this Northern model was slowly adopted in the South in order to restore the racial control lost with the abolition of slavery. At first this de facto segregation was enforced by social custom, but later its policies of proscription and disenfranchisement were enacted into the de jure segregation of the infamous Jim Crow laws. According to Woodward, these laws were the direct result of a growing political and social solidarity among whites. "Just as the Negro gained his emancipation and new rights through a falling out between white men, he now stood to lose his rights through the reconciliation of white men."[123]

While those who formulated the equal protection clause of the Fourteenth Amendment thus obviously wanted justice for blacks, they just as obviously did not intend to strike down segregation. Hence to formulate intent by restricting it to the contemporary outlook of the legislators is clearly not the right way to formulate it. We must therefore choose today at what level to read the framers' intentions. Some larger conviction of principle must be attributed to them, such as the overall intention to outlaw discrimination on the basis of race, or, more broadly still, on the basis of any form of official prejudice. Here, of course, is where a particular judicial philosophy comes into play. Choosing an intent to outlaw discrimination on the basis of race would be sufficient to deal with the segregation issue of *Brown*, but not sufficient to use the Fourteenth Amendment to protect women or homosexuals. The level of generality of intent that an individual justice chooses thus becomes crucial.[124]

Hence there are really two judicial choices involved in any constitutional decision: the formulation of original intent in terms of a general principle and the application of that principle to the facts of a particular case. What determines these two judicial choices? Ultimately the moral values and political preferences of individual judges, who must use these preferences to fill in the temporal ellipses between the words of the Constitution, the conventions of judicial tradition, and the particular question currently litigated. Competent and responsible judges will naturally disagree about the results of both types of choices. Conservative judges will be much less influenced than liberal judges by the interplay between current societal realities, the demands of social justice, and minority rights. As strict constructionists, they will interpret the Constitution narrowly, so as to make as little change in the law as possible.

Both conservatives and liberals would agree, for example, that only Congress, not the Supreme Court, should make law when the Constitution is silent, but they might well disagree on whether or not in a given matter the Constitution is indeed silent. Is there a right of privacy contained in the wording of the Fourteenth Amendment? If so, how fundamental is it? Is it to be extended by judicial discretion only to certain matters of intimate concern, freeing only these matters and not others from surveillance by government? Will it protect homosexual conduct? Is it broad enough to encompass a woman's decision to terminate her pregnancy? "The truth is," concludes one federal judge who has tried seriously to grapple with these issues, "that no litmus test exists by which judges can confidently and consistently measure the constitutionality of their decisions." Justice Brennan has also spoken of this "ambiguity inherent in the effort" to apply constitutional ideals to modern circumstances. "We current Justices read the Constitution in the only way we can: as 20th century Americans. We look to the history of the time of framing and the intervening history of interpretation. But the ultimate question must be, what do the words of the text mean in our time."[125]

But there is nonetheless a limit to this power of judicial review, because ultimately the Constitution is a document belonging to the nation as a whole. "There is always the risk," a senior federal judge once observed, "that persons start with the totally false assumption that the Constitution is the province of the lawyers. . . . Moreover, I think it is quite clear that there is a grave danger that if we think of the Constitution exclusively in terms of constitutional law, we shall lose some of its most important symbolic, as well as practical, values to our society."[126] Hence there can well develop at certain times a popular consensus that the Court is badly executing its role to interpret traditional or emerging political practices in terms of constitutional ideals.

This actually happened when the Court tried to halt the emergence of our limited welfare state during the first third of this century. As we saw earlier, federal courts at that time regularly invalidated minimum wage and maximum hour laws, as well as child labor laws, in an effort to protect the contract and property rights of employers. In principle these rights were guaranteed by the Constitution, but their laissez-faire tone and character eventually came into conflict with newer social imperatives favoring government regulation of the economy and the redistribution of wealth. In the late 1930s the Supreme Court resolved this conflict by abruptly changing its legal outlook on social legislation. Its earlier views on the kind of nation the Constitution wanted us to be yielded to a new national consensus regarding a more active role for government. This is perhaps the most visible recent example of the Court's anchoring itself in society. In the end such anchoring constitutes the greatest safeguard for the authority and legitimacy of its decisions.

This brings us to the third reason that the establishment clause will most likely remain a riddle in the years ahead: many of the Court's decisions in this area still sit, in William Lee Miller's felicitous phrase, "partly undigested on the nation's stomach."[127] The general culture, in other words, is still too deeply divided on matters of religion. We have already discussed many of the reasons for this division. The net result is that separation of religion and government continues to weigh less for us as a nation than the free exercise of religion, and insofar as government fosters the latter, the line of separation is going to get blurred. In deciding where this line is to be drawn in any future situation, therefore, it is unlikely that the Court will ever again allow the religious freedom concept to be swallowed up by the separation concept. Justice Sandra Day O'Connor implied as much when she wrote in 1985 of the Court's future agenda: "The solution to the conflict between the Religion Clauses lies in identifying workable limits to the government's license to promote the free exercise of religion."[128]

While this division in the general culture is to a certain extent the inevitable result of the various ellipses that still persist, it is important to recognize its positive side. Neither the Court's understanding of disestablishment nor that of society has ever produced the type of gap that would engender moral conflict. There is not now, in other words, nor has there ever been, any moral ellipsis. Had this been otherwise, had disestablishment actually raised moral issues, the conscience of the nation would surely have been more taut from the start, as it was on questions like slavery, segregation, and racial inequality. Instead, disestablishment was usually left morally unfocused, in the limbo of law and history, fluctuating back and forth like any other political or cultural phenomenon.

In spite of this absence of moral conflict, however, the country as a whole still stubbornly resists consensus either on how government should relate to religion or on how religion should function in society. Nor is this situation likely to change. We are talking, it should be remembered, about a nation where there are not only secularists and Christians — fundamentalist, liberal, and moderate — all thinking differently, but where by the year 2000 there are likely to be as many Moslems as Jews. As for the intent of the Founders, it seems fairly clear that most Americans would draw the line of separation tighter than they originally intended. While citizens today generally believe they should keep the Founders' thinking in view, they are also aware that that thinking differs in very significant ways from their own.

At the same time it is also clear that there is at present relatively little support in the country for that absolute separation proposed by the Supreme Court in 1947. In that year the justices began their establishment clause odyssey with the *Everson* case, erroneously attributing to the framers the separation convictions put into effect by Jefferson and Madison in Virginia. While we now know that these convictions did not necessarily belong to everyone who formulated and ratified the First Amendment, we are also aware today that we will probably never know with certitude what they actually meant by the words of the establishment clause. "Original intention" can thus only be ascertained by subsequent interpretation.

Recognition of this *Everson* mistake seems to have been one of the main reasons for the Court's developing its accommodation doctrine. We shall have to wait for some time, however, before seeing where the doctrine finally leads. As for the nationalization issue, the question is not whether the Court will ever exempt the states from complying with federal establishment policy (which would be quite unrealistic), but whether the tenuous nexus of this clause to the Fourteenth Amendment (in contrast to that of the free exercise clause) may perhaps prompt the justices to allow more leeway in the future for local initiative to deal with local conflict.

Finally, we must not forget that we have been discussing a body of constitutional law less than fifty years old, and any speculation regarding popular consensus has to take that fact into account. If we place these Court decisions on disestablishment in the context of a legal tradition more than two hundred years old, it is obvious that they do not yet possess cultural longevity. The justices are empowered to give the language of the First Amendment the meaning they choose, guided by their responsibility to the historical text, their understandings of historical purpose, the presuppositions of society, and the felt needs of the day. But finally their decisions have to be legitimized by the religious experience of the nation as a whole, since this

The Riddle of the Establishment Clause   115

experience is what undergirds the constitutional principle of free exercise and disestablishment. The axiom of Justice Holmes is very much to the point: "The life of the law has not been logic: it has been experience."[129]

Experience was indeed at the heart of the whole enterprise from the start. It was a "fair experiment," said Jefferson, seventeen years after the adoption of the religion clauses, one that solved "the great and interesting question whether freedom of religion is compatible with order in government."[130] Religious voluntarism followed this legal separation from government and fostered in turn an extraordinary intermeshing of religion and society. This led eventually to the religious and moral pluralism of our time as well as to new inquiry today into religion's role in society and government's role in religion. Future stages in this experiment and this experience are therefore inevitable.

The problem, as one legal scholar has pointed out, is that "in the legal system... everything gets classified. Religion becomes a category, and categories are easy to manipulate. A sense of the hard, living reality of religion for believers—the sense that they believe that they are responding to a living transcendent intelligent Being—is easy to lose."[131] To what extent will the Court succeed in the future in preventing such loss? The justices are surely not going to find this challenge any easier in the case of new developments than they did in the case of older ones. In 1963 Justice Clark admitted that "interpretation of a delicate sort" was needed before the Court could know in a given case how to be neutral.[132] Justice White candidly acknowledged this again in 1980, and his words suggest to us that the riddle will likely go unsolved into the indefinite future:

> Establishment Clause cases are not easy; they stir deep feelings; and we are divided among ourselves, perhaps reflecting the different views on this subject of the people of this country.

What is certain is that our decisions have tended to avoid categorical imperatives and absolutist approaches at either end of the range of possible outcomes. This course sacrifices clarity and predictability for flexibility, but this promises to be the case until the continuing interaction between the courts and states produces a single, more-encompassing construction of the Establishment Clause.[133]

PART III
EDUCATION'S PRISM

EDUCATION, NO LESS THAN law and religion, is a beleaguered institution in America today. The surprising popularity of three critical studies published almost simultaneously in 1987 testifies to the widespread sense that all is not well in the republic and that what we are doing in our schools is somehow making it worse. I refer, of course, to Allan Bloom's *The Closing of the American Mind*, E. D. Hirsch, Jr.'s *Cultural Literacy*, and Ernest L. Boyer's *College*. Though widely different in scope, outlook, and contribution to the educational enterprise, all three focus on the large and essentially cultural question of what it means to be an educated citizen. While Boyer and Hirsch are generally hopeful that some changes in the system can rectify past mistakes, Bloom is in angry despair that anything can really be done anymore to humanize college students, even the best ones, or to give them any understanding at all of the cultural legacy of the West.

Bloom and Hirsch deal explicitly with the role of religious values in the American educational process. Hirsch and Boyer, while not enthusiasts for a role for law in this area, nevertheless make measured recommendations for some government control in instituting change. For all three, however, the curriculum of our schools is a truly public issue, to be debated in public by citizens searching for the common good of their respective communities. "Our thought and our politics have become inexorably bound up with the universities," says Bloom. "This is the

American moment in world history, the one for which we shall be forever judged."[1]

These studies touched such a sensitive nerve in 1987 because so many in the country were already anxious and apprehensive about the young. What were they learning? What did they know about the world and especially about the nation that their elders were handing on to them? Widely publicized reports are today informing these worried elders that 23 million Americans have been identified as functionally illiterate, which means that they read at a level below that of the average fourth-grader. The majority of these are white, moreover, not members of minority groups. In a 1986 assessment of almost 8,000 seventeen-year-olds, it was found that one in five did not know that George Washington commanded the army during the American Revolution, and almost one in three did not know that Lincoln wrote the Emancipation Proclamation. Thirty percent of these teenagers did not know that Columbus reached the New World before 1750 or that the Watergate scandal occurred after 1950.[2]

Widespread public concern about such statistics, as well as about the functioning of higher education generally, is more than justified. One does not have to subscribe to the shrill barrages of former Education Secretary William J. Bennett to recognize that the United States is finding itself at a loss to perform well the task of every culture to pass on to the next generation the values, skills, and knowledge shared and held in respect by the present generation. "A Nation at Risk" was the title of the 1983 commentary by the National Commission on Excellence in Education. Written at the request of then Education Secretary Terrel Bell, this report unexpectedly turned out to be a call to arms, propelling education into a national political issue that continues today to arouse legislators and the general public at local, state, and federal levels.

Everyone now seems to recognize education for what it is and has always been: a prism. Prisms are transparent triangular-shaped bodies of glass used to disperse light into its component colors: whatever one sees through them looks different. The educational experience acts in the same way. It functions as a medium, dispersing knowledge into its components and altering permanently the way students see themselves and their world. Hence the way we as a people think about this experience and discourse on its content will necessarily have massive significance for our national life. As one manifestation of those two large phenomena of our society, our pluralism and our concern for the common good, education is at least as important an institution as law and religion. Indeed, the boundaries of all three overlap at times and also periodically change. At present we are in the midst of just such a boundary change in education.

In the pages that follow I want to develop four affirmations regarding education at the college and university level. First, very significant consequences follow from the fact that we as a people have decided to make available to all Americans in principle the extraordinary capacity of higher education to initiate students into their roles as mature and intelligent citizens. Secondly, and as a result of this goal, higher education's current skepticism and intellectual restlessness is becoming much more diffused in society than in former times, and this has wrongfully prompted the current agitation to return our colleges and universities to the less disturbing certainties of their past. Thirdly, the two risks that really do threaten our institutions of higher learning, those of elitism and value neutrality, are insufficiently recognized today and therefore badly guarded against. Finally, because law and religion, each in its own way, address these risks, their boundaries inevitably interconnect with higher education at that point where all three have begun to search for the common good.

1. Initiation into Citizenship

We need to begin with a brief look at history. Since classical times "liberal education" in its broad sense has been understood as the education of the well-informed citizen. For Aristotle it was a political concept, the education that a free-born citizen required in order to play an active part in the life of his or her city. Aristotle defined its goal in his *Politics* as knowing how to govern like a free person and how to obey like a free person. The content of liberal education, as Aristotle also noted, will thus differ according to the particular form of culture and government under which a citizen lives. It involves the passing on of a spiritual heritage from one generation to the next, those values and ideals—religious, philosophic, artistic, scientific—which are seen as worthy of esteem and are therefore accepted and lived by a given community.

Plato made the same point in his *Laws* when speaking of the ideal of Greek education, *areté*. This word's normal English translation, "virtue," is correct but inadequate in an educational context, since in this context *areté* carried larger meanings for the Greeks, that of "general excellence" when applied to private life and that of "good citizenship" when applied to public life. Hence Plato could say that "we must take education from childhood to mean the teaching of *areté*, a training which produces a keen desire to become a perfect citizen, who knows how to rule and be ruled as justice demands." The classic ideal of education was consequently one focused on a public community purpose, namely good citizenship, the means whereby a given culture perpetuates its way of life.[3]

This classic aim of education was radically modified at the time of the Renaissance by the humanists, who wanted education for citizenship to be explicitly related to the formation of character and to the reform of church and society. Humanists in the fifteenth, sixteenth, and seventeenth centuries, shunning the abstractions of philosophy, wanted students formed in good taste and right values, and oriented toward responsible public action. The reforms they proposed for education were the primary instruments for the reform of society. The humanists thus added to the goal of education for good citizenship the goal of education for self-fulfillment: they wanted citizens who were also good people.[4]

These two distinct traditions in liberal education have followed a line down to our own time, though their distinctness may not be readily discernible in their modern context. The Greek tradition still emphasizes freedom of intellectual search rather than content in learning, encouraging skepticism and toleration of conflicting beliefs. Its appeal is to the specialized research of the natural sciences, the social sciences, and mathematics, and its natural home is the great research universities of today. The Renaissance tradition, on the other hand, still emphasizes the crucial importance of traditional learning communities to train for leadership. Its appeal is primarily to the humanities, to literature, philosophy, history, and religion, whose great classic texts are studied in order to encourage the true virtues of citizenship. Its natural home today is the small liberal arts colleges, especially those with strong religious traditions, and its continual challenge is to guard itself from idolatry of the past.[5]

Neither of these two educational traditions, it should be noted, has ever been divorced from preparing students for a career. The issue for both has rather been how best to do this, how best to help adolescents achieve adulthood in their society, and their common tool has always been expansion of the mind. While the making of human personality obviously includes a broader group of objectives than intellectual growth, such growth was nevertheless thought to be fundamental to all others at a mature level, for it is precisely this that enlarges students' capacity for conscious living, extends the reach and range of their relationships, and enables them to take possession of the world around them. In this way they are prepared to play a more useful and significant role in the social world of their generation and consequently contribute a greater share to the achievement of their community.

Each of these traditions recognizes that very specialized instruction in certain skills may well assume great importance in such career preparation. Alfred North Whitehead, a great humanist philosopher as well as a great mathematician, saw this with admirable clarity. "The antithesis between a technical and a liberal education is fallacious," he wrote in his seminal *The Aims of Education*. "There can be no adequate technical education which is not liberal, and no liberal education which is not technical: that is, no education which does not impart both technique and intellectual vision. In simpler language, education should turn out the pupil with something he knows well and something he can do well.... The intellect does not work best in a vacuum." Whitehead had no tolerance at all for educational pedantry. "Of course, education should be useful, whatever your aim in life.... It is useful because understanding is useful."[6] It constitutes, in other words, a durable consumer good.

Because American education is heir to both these intellectual traditions, it has always sought, at least as an ideal, to provide a curriculum that balances the humanities, which focus on the human condition, with the natural and social sciences, which focus on the processes of nature and the structures of society. All three involve technical skills of some sort, though this type of specialization is a long way from purely vocational training. The higher the education the more these will be skills of the mind, such as quantitative analysis or a facility in language and communication. At the undergraduate level, however, such skills aim less at producing the specialist than the balanced personality. Educators are well aware, for example, that there can be just as much creativity in developing laboratory skills as in the experiences of a humanities class. Indeed, vigorous training in skills of the mind can probably be better achieved in disciplines whose study is organized sequentially, in increasing depth, around established bodies of knowledge. This is why success in differential equations or inorganic chemistry generally reveals more about a student's sheer competence than completing a course in eighteenth-century English literature.

But liberal education, and especially the humanities, has always sought to move beyond the mere acquisition of intellectual skills and to grasp the discipline's meaning for one's life as a person in society. This search for meaning has recently come to the center of the American educational scene, partly as a reaction to the tendency in the recent past to focus the entire educational process on its vocational end-result. This tendency has come to be seen as inadequate to prepare a person to grapple either with the complex machinery of society or with the novelty of contemporary technology. An electronic enmeshing of humankind is taking place today, creating very different experiences of interpersonal communication and very different perspectives on life generally. Educated persons must not only provide more specialized answers but also ask larger questions about what George Kennan has called "the entire product of humanity's past efforts in the development of a civilized life, that product of which we are the beneficiaries and without which our lives would have no meaning."[7]

This makes it essential to place a much greater emphasis upon human values at every point in the educational process, lest personal existence become increasingly depersonalized. We shall have more to say later on about this central question of values. For the present it suffices to note the connection of values to that deepest desire of students for their own self-fulfillment, their search to find themselves completely in all their natural powers and capacities, especially through interpersonal relationships.

This making of themselves, intellectually, morally, socially, has always appeared to men and women as their greatest achievement, and it is perhaps the major preoccupation of American youth during their undergraduate years. What they seek foremost is some ultimate frame of reference for the countless intellectual and emotional stimuli involved in the maturing process called college, some subjective integration of all those vital forces which the development of their natural powers has suddenly released within them. But all these efforts are radically a matter of free decisions for values in every phase of their personal existence.

The whole thrust of liberal education is thus to provide and support convictions regarding what is ultimately good and valuable in life, convictions which are in turn able to judge and criticize those larger questions of human conduct and development now confronting our society. The great threat we face as a nation is that our fate may be in the hands of narrowly educated technicians, who may know systems analysis but may not prize justice, nor have the slightest inclination to seek the common good, the good of the species, the good of civilization. "It is something infinitely greater and more important than we are," says George Kennan; "it is the whole; we are only a part.... It was bestowed upon us; and it was bestowed upon us with the implicit obligation to cherish it, to preserve it, to develop it, to pass it on — let us hope improved, but in any case intact — to the others who were supposed to come after us."[8]

Now both the glory and the bane of American education is that it has sought to democratize this ideal of liberal education, to infuse it into our entire educational system. In doing so we have opened ourselves, as no other nation has, to the endless quest of devising programs for an enormously diverse population. We want to encourage learning for its own sake in all college curricula; at the same time we feel acute responsibility to prepare students for the practicalities of life. The result has been an uneasy balance in almost all our institutions. Some of them will stress the life of the mind and the joys of free intellectual inquiry; others will focus on preparation for pursuit of a career. Some will have missions that are concise and clearly articulated; others will endlessly struggle to formulate their role in their particular communities; still others will not aim at any sharp focus at all.

What is common to all these efforts is a conviction that there are universal human needs that have to be addressed by undergraduate education and that these should be made available to students from a wide variety of social situations. Sheer numbers magnify the complexity of this conviction. Between 1960 and 1983 undergraduate enrollments trebled in the United States, growing from 3,227,000 to 9,707,000. The chief source of this expansion was the increase in the proportion of young people going to college during this period, from 34 percent to 58 percent. Most of this growth, moreover, took place in local community colleges and state college systems, the burden of the educational process consequently falling disproportionately on them. The number of colleges themselves increased by 60 percent during the same period, up to a total of almost 3,000 institutions.[9]

What has become absolutely clear, then, is that as a nation we are no longer seeking to reach and teach the academically talented elite. We want the benefits of intellectual growth and of a more fully human moral and social life to be available in principle to all Americans. The obvious perils of charting such a course will eventually be balanced, we believe, by the achievement of its egalitarian goal. In the meantime, however, the whole enterprise has opened itself to a seemingly endless series of studies seeking to diagnose the good and bad effects of higher education on this startling diversity of students. In 1984–1985, for example, there were three major critiques, all different in their emphases but with the same essential message: our colleges have become too utilitarian, too vocational, and too parochial in their world outlook, with their "supermarket" curricula in a state of incoherence and disarray. All three studies warned of the serious deficiency in student knowledge of world affairs, especially the role of the United States on the international scene.[10]

Boyer, Hirsch, and Bloom also focus on this failure of school curricula to cohere. Boyer argues that "the undergraduate college, the very heart of higher learning, is a troubled institution" whose failure to decide upon an integrated "core" of subjects points to a loss of faith in general education.[11] He is troubled most by his finding that faculty at many institutions no longer debate what knowledge is essential in order for someone to be considered an educated person. This is the knowledge that Hirsch calls "cultural literacy," which he finds seriously deficient at the levels of elementary and secondary education. He is talking, he insists, about the mainstream cultural vocabulary of America, not some exclusive WASP culture of the elite schools. "Literate culture is the most democratic culture in our land; it excludes nobody; it cuts across generations and social groups and classes;... beyond the narrow spheres of family, neighborhood, and region."[12]

Allan Bloom's book, about which we shall say more presently, espouses an even more fundamentalist notion of curriculum as a fixed body of canonized texts from which we appropriate culture as we would from the tour of a museum. It seems to be utterly beyond Bloom's ken that curriculum in contemporary colleges, widely diverse as these are, socially, economically, and geographically, simply cannot be immune to the chaos and terror that impact modern life. He deplores the influence on the university of the civil rights movement, the war in Vietnam, affirmative action, feminism, rock music, and most of our other social upheavals, as if the educational ideal were hermetically to seal off both students and faculty from such events. As one perceptive critic has noted, the

"Bloomian university does not see itself as having any practical social aim, even the aim of educating citizens so that they will govern their own ethical lives better and more reflectively. For according to Bloom the aim of the 'highest life' is to depart from the ethical and social life altogether."[13]

I do not wish to imply that these books have nothing valuable to say about curriculum. Bloom rightly points to the bad effects of certain innovations of the 1960s, when grading was softened and credit began to be given in courses for "personal growth." Boyer's insights and recommendations are especially sensitive to those historical developments that are the real sources of the problem. For the reasons cited by Boyer and those developed by Hirsch, there is now a significant discontinuity between the earlier education of undergraduates and present expectations of college faculty. Boyer notes also that too much emphasis has been placed on institutional mission at the two extremes of the educational spectrum, that of the land-grant and community colleges to emphasize vocational training and that of the graduate schools to turn out professional scholars. The result in each has too often been that large humanist concerns have been either squeezed into courses in skills and technique or fragmented into highly specialized research.

The point I am making, therefore, is not that there are no problems or need for balance in higher education, but rather that, given its extraordinary diversity as well as the tumultuous character of our present national scene, we should really not expect coherence to be the curriculum norm. For society creates the prism through which society is seen, and its refracted light illumines the extraordinary diversity of its citizens' interests, assumptions, and values. However desirable coherence may be in the abstract, we ought to presume, unless shown otherwise, that in concrete institutions coherence will usually yield to disagreement and conflict. Far from being the result of a loss of educational nerve or a surrender to mediocrity, such disagreement and conflict should rather be seen as an authentic expression of sincerely held convictions and a symbol of vigorous university life — a sign not of malaise but of health. Not to acknowledge the legitimacy of this situation is seriously to undervalue the democratic reach and toleration of American liberal education, as well as its openness to the impact of cultural change.

2. Tolerating the Ambiguity of Knowledge

What we have just said — with qualified approval — about diversity, disagreement, tolerance, and openness in American liberal education constitutes the basis for Allan Bloom's caustic charge that this same education is responsible not for expanding but for closing the student mind. Openness today, he says, is not openness to knowledge and certitude, but really a synonym for indifference, a total unconcern for any shared goals or common vision. Teachers are convinced and students are taught that all conceptions of the good human life are equally valid and that any attempt at rational criticism of particular beliefs is an expression of unenlightened prejudice. "Openness used to be the virtue that permitted us to seek the good by using reason. It now means accepting everything and denying reason's power.... Science's latest attempts to grasp the human situation — cultural relativism, historicism, the fact-value distinction — are the suicide of science.... Openness to closedness is what we teach."[14]

Besides these attacks on science, both natural and social, there is a concern throughout Bloom's book for the corrosive effect of relativism on students' respect for the true nature of democratic government. The principles of natural rights and self-evident truth are now casually ignored, says Bloom. "All such teachers of openness had either no interest in or were actively hostile to the Declaration of Independence and the Constitution."[15] Although his immediate target is higher education, his tirade is mainly derivative: his real target is American society as a whole. In this I think he is dead wrong. He is especially wrong about two aspects of our society that he singles out for comment, namely our democratic tradition and our scientific achievement. There is indeed a relativism that is integral to both, but its source is not indifference to truth but a recognition of the imperfection and ambiguity of all knowledge. This relativism has not "impoverished the souls of today's students," as Bloom's subtitle proclaims, but has in fact enriched them.

Let us first look more closely at our democratic tradition of natural rights and equality under law. *E Pluribus Unum* was the motto chosen for the Great Seal of the United States by Adams, Franklin, and Jefferson: out of many colonies one republic. The implications of this pluralism were recognized from the start. Though we may think and act differently as citizens, we have nevertheless decided to live our lives together in a single nation. A bitter civil war is testimony that our diversity can be contained in that unity. While certain rights are believed to be possessed by all and guaranteed by law, there is no specific obligatory content in our culture as a whole. In consequence local cultures abound and religious denominations flourish as a matter of legal principle, thereby promoting throughout the country a plurality of ethical and moral systems. The Supreme Court has explicitly recognized the compatibility of this pluralism with the academic integrity of higher education: any group of citizens, regardless of their religious commitment, has a right to government support for the secular goals of their schools.[16]

"If there is any fixed star in our constitutional constellation," said Justice Robert Jackson for the Court in 1943, "it is that no official, high or petty, can prescribe what shall be orthodox in politics, nationalism, religion, or other matters of opinion, or force citizens to confess by word or act their faith therein."[17] A generation earlier Justice Oliver Wendell Holmes, Jr., sounded a broader principle. Intolerance comes naturally to us, he said, but as a people we have learned by experience that intolerance does not pay. In America men and women have

> come to believe even more than they believe the very foundations of their own conduct that the ultimate good derived is better reached by free trade in ideas—that the best test of truth is the power of the thought to get itself accepted in the competition of the market, and that truth is the only ground upon which their wishes safely can be carried out. That at any rate is the theory of our Constitution. It is an experiment as all life is an experiment. Every year if not every day we have to wager our salvation upon some prophesy based upon imperfect knowledge.[18]

"Belief," "wager," "salvation," "prophesy," "imperfect knowledge" — this is not the language of science or even of law, but of myth, reflecting an attitude toward the free expression of ideas not unlike that of a religious act of faith. This commitment, said Judge Learned Hand, "presupposes that right conclusions are more likely to be gathered out of a multitude of tongues, than through any kind of authoritative selection. To many this is, and always will be, folly; but we have staked upon it our all."[19] This same language of belief and risk appears in the classic formulation of Jefferson "that truth is great and will prevail if left to herself; that she is the proper and sufficient antagonist of error, and has nothing to fear from the conflict unless by human interposition disarmed of her natural weapons, free argument and debate."[20]

These words of Jefferson highlight a very important implication of this American commitment to pluralism of idea and discourse: each citizen must have some standards for judging what is error and what is not. These standards may indeed be socially derived and socially mediated, but in the end they become convictions of the individual. For in a democracy the presumption is that, because it is possible to distinguish between truth and falsehood, citizens must test their thinking before they speak, in order to judge for themselves whether or not it is false. Such testing will inevitably result in conflicting views of truth, and this is why the crucial factor will always be "the power of the thought to get itself accepted in the competition of the market." Alexander Meiklejohn has pointed out that these conflicting views have to be expressed, not because each is equally valid, but because each is relevant: everything worth saying ought to be said. If a view is responsibly held by anyone, it should be heard. "To be afraid of ideas, any idea, is to be unfit for self government."[21]

The problem is, of course, as many fear, including Allan Bloom, that the marketplace may turn into a bullring, that ideas of racism, segregation, genocide, and fascism may eventually impose themselves. Yet our First Amendment guarantee of free expression says that unless such ideas incite violence, coercion, or the violation of law, they may not be restricted. The risk here, then, is that speech which is true may indeed be unable to survive speech which is false. But the alternative is to trust, not in the give and take of public discourse, but what is acceptable and unacceptable to the few who for a moment hold enough power to tyrannize over the many.[22] The first risk we have taken, the second we reject. For the American commitment is a wager, "an experiment as all life is an experiment," bringing with it ambiguity and ambivalence as well as truth. To many it is folly, "but we have staked upon it our all."

Democracy succeeds, then, insofar as all voices, especially the marginal, are included in its conversation. Its commitment to truth is pluralist, and pluralism always tends to be messy and to promote conflict. From the public standpoint, therefore, questions about the good human life must always be raised but will rarely be settled. This is the world American students must be taught to live in, not some past age when there may have been more public harmony but less public education. Obviously it cannot be demonstrated that our society, based on these convictions, is better than another, just as the self-evident truths of the Declaration of Independence cannot be demonstrated. We take a chance when we commit ourselves to the results of free expression, confident that these results, however unpleasant they may be at any given moment, will eventually promote the general good of society.

Such a "faith," it should be noted, is relatively new in the world. Peoples in past ages had very different understandings of what it means to be human in society. Even today such faith is denied in theory and in practice by much of humanity most of the time. Nor does our First Amendment guarantee point the way finally to unambiguous decision, but rather to compromise and accommodation. We have confidence, however, that in the midst of public conflict the nation's legal process will keep the system itself in equilibrium until such time as some long-range consensus begins to emerge. In other words, in a democracy such as ours conflict must be recognized as having a positive value because it can give rise to moral judgments which are as close to the practical truth as we can get.

Public diversity and disagreement should therefore be welcomed, not feared, as long as the parties to the dispute are committed to resolving the conflict and adjusting their prior claims in the light of the public argument. If, however, either party is so committed to one possible outcome that it is unwilling to consider any alternative, then of course the particular conflict cannot be creative at all and no new possibilities for the community can be realized. It ought to be clear to students, therefore, that harmony is not the ideal pattern of public relationships in American society. They must not grow into adulthood reluctant to seek resolution of conflict through argument and compromise. For knowing and learning are communal experiences. But such conflict can be creative of the common good only if there is initial acceptance of the possibility that one's own knowledge of truth may be partial. The pluralism of our moral discourse, in short, is not a solvent of our national unity, but the precise mode by which we live and work and think and cooperate together.

The fact that our democratic tradition has always embraced diversity and taught tolerance thus inevitably relativizes all beliefs in the public realm. But such relativism presumes that these beliefs, whether religious, moral, or political, will be argued forcefully and with conviction, and that this argument will issue in commitment, not indifference. Allan Bloom does not really believe this, because he sees the public argument constantly changing, its substance often without closure. For Bloom is a classicist thinker and, like all classicists, views historical change as somehow accidental to life. Beneath such change all things have very specific and unchanging natures, with their truths immutable and capable of being known with certitude. In the classicist view it is the patient investigation of these natures that is the proper object of university education. Bloom's lament is thus for modernity's skepticism of such certainties and for the general sensitivity today to the relativity and incompleteness of knowledge.

To get a better perspective here, let us look for a moment at another of Bloom's targets, the natural and social sciences. He is loath to recognize the importance of these disciplines for liberal education because each in its own way accepts this relativity of knowledge. Yet understanding science and its influence upon modernity is precisely the way for students to understand why they tend to think the way they do and why their ingrained search for the true and the good need not be thwarted nor threatened by the loss of certitudes.

Classical physics, for example, claimed to measure quantities that had objective existence, while in modern physics the concept of relativity makes what we know of physical objects depend on whatever else is in their "frame of reference." This demands recognition that truths about physical realities can be formulated in various ways, each formulation being true relative to the observer making the measurements and to the context in which they are made. Einstein's concern for the astronomically large distances of outer space was followed by Werner Heisenberg's for the infinitesimally shorter ones in the atom. His Uncertainty Principle formulated the relativity of our knowledge of the subatomic world: either the location of an atomic particle or its velocity can be measured precisely, but not both at the same time. Hence the more we know of the one the less we know of the other. Science thus gives us not a picture of nature so much as a picture of our relationship to nature. As instruments observing the movement of electrons differ, so will the observation: "the observation plays a decisive role in the event and the reality varies, depending on whether we observe it or not."[23] We are, in other words, part of that process of nature we observe. We do not see things in themselves but only aspects of things. Our very act of observing disturbs and alters the observed.

This concept of relativity in physics, like that of evolution in biology, has had enormous psychological and epistemological consequences. While the original application of these discoveries was to very specific scientific fields, they soon brought to the twentieth century a promise of far more general validity, one that eventually came to be tested by many other disciplines. Today's historians no longer claim they can be totally disinterested observers of the past. They recognize the need to interpret historical data in order to understand it at all, thereby taking the subjective into account much more seriously than earlier scholars. This does not rule out their knowing the past with certitude, but it qualifies that certitude: all historical knowledge is inevitably colored by present experience. "We are all linguistic, historical, social beings," says

David Tracy, "struggling for some new interpretation of ourselves, our language, history, society and culture."[24]

History's qualified relativity regarding knowledge of the past is paralleled by anthropology's caution in dealing with the value relativity of various cultures. This discipline's cultural relativism rests on the empirical premise that in fact ethical values differ between one culture and another. But anthropologists do not claim this premise to be an ethical principle, merely a methodological tool from which their discipline as such draws no moral corollary. Hence they leave to ethicists the responsibility of articulating a rationale for moral values. Very few ethicists, on the other hand, would say that no objective way exists to justify basic ethical judgments, or that different judgments are simply the result of different emotions and feelings. Those ethicists who do say this are respected for their challenging theories but have very limited credibility among peers. "The chief value of [ethical] relativism," says one authority, "is that, by drawing attention to cultural diversity, it has brought philosophers to distinguish between moral rules, etc., and laws of nature, and has encouraged a critical appraisal of the grounds offered for divergent moral judgments."[25]

From the current moral pluralism in the United States, therefore, it does not follow that everyone thinks that their morality is based on purely subjective preferences with no reasoned foundation, any more than the nation's religious pluralism means that for the beliefs of religious people. Both these pluralisms are part of our ethos. Because such relativism is in the cultural air, it will inevitably be refracted in education's prism. Hence undergraduates need to be taught how to get behind both these pluralisms to the convictions that sustain and motivate them. While they learn to be critical of certainties, they should become skeptical of all relativisms as well. Our moral principles are part of our lived experience and will therefore be found embodied in our conventions, customs, beliefs, rituals, and institutions. If educators do their work properly, this critical sense, far from diminishing in the country, should become even more evident, because higher education is expanding so rapidly. Of itself, therefore, this situation does not entail moral chaos or the "anything goes" mentality, but rather tolerance for the diversity of moral discourse, something extremely difficult if not impossible for the classicist educator to accept.

None of what I have said is meant to minimize the troubled concern of large numbers of Americans today for the state of our higher education. Allan Bloom has successfully tapped into this concern and reflected it back with confident pessimism. He knows very well that as a people we are able to tolerate pluralism in religious belief much more easily than pluralism in moral practice. This is probably because there is something in all of us that wants our external lives and those of our neighbors to be clear-cut and orderly and that resists the messy confusion of the contemporary scene. But as John Kenneth Galbraith reminded us when he characterized our century over a decade ago, we live in "the age of uncertainty," where we all must seek our own constants. "In the last century capitalists were certain of the success of capitalism, socialists of socialism, imperialists of colonialism, and the ruling classes knew they were meant to rule. Little of this certainty now survives. Given the dismaying complexity of the problems mankind now faces, it would surely be odd if it did."[26]

Shortly after Galbraith wrote this, contemporary historian Richard Barnet did a series of articles on world resources for the *New Yorker*. "The promise of the industrial age," he wrote, "has been accompanied by many disappointments, but none so devastating as the growing belief that civilization is out of control." One of his underlying themes was that citizens the world over are losing faith in the quality, leadership, and integrity of such basic institutions as government, education, church, and family."[27]

Can we expect our colleges and universities to ignore these tensions or explain them away? Is their task not precisely to grapple with them and to see to it that their students understand their history and meaning? Nor can this be simply a matter of what books are read and taught (as Bloom would have it). The root problem is how academics and their students are now to relate to knowledge. Too much in modern science, philosophy, anthropology, and religion has changed that relationship in recent years, and no amount of public authority or parental disquiet will enable us to recover the old boundaries and limits of the known. In the past we may well have been certain of too much. The risk we have to avoid today is becoming too certain of our uncertainties.

3. Elitism and Value Neutrality

Liberal education in America has traditionally sought to prepare students for citizenship and, at the university level, to equip them with the critical sense needed to understand their country's history, values, achievements, and goals. Pluralism is now a hallmark of their country, powerfully affecting relationships between family, government, religion, and the workplace. Hence we should not be surprised to find it reflected in the outlook of the students themselves, since their preferences, behavior, and academic performance will naturally tend to mirror conditions in society as a whole. When we speak of the quality and content of their higher education, therefore, what we are really asking is how they are being prepared to cope with these conditions. It is in this context that I see a double problem to be faced by educators: not the risk of relativism but the risk of elitism; not value plurality but value neutrality. Let us look more closely at this double problem.

The issue of elitism was brought home to me several years ago by a stark scene from the movie version of William Styron's novel *Sophie's Choice*. Sophie is led by a guard through the mud of the Nazi concentration camp, past a long cellblock of desperate prisoners pleading loudly for food. As she enters the enclosed area that houses the commandant and his family, the camera rises behind her and we get in full view a beautiful cottage surrounded by trees and lawn, with a garden, a swing, and a young child playing. Inside the house the camera shows us two intelligent women discussing domestic matters in a typical suburban atmosphere. The commandant, we learn, is a person of some education and culture who is bored with his present assignment and is impatiently awaiting promotion. His wife is concerned about her husband's career; their young daughter is concerned that the next camp may not have such good opportunities as this one for play and games. No one has the slightest concern for the horror which we have just been witnessing beyond the gate.

This scene highlights a deficiency of higher education that has only gradually emerged into contemporary consciousness, namely its tendency to isolate both student and institution from the ordinary life of the desperate, the poor, and the exploited. In *College* Ernest Boyer speaks of the "disturbing gap" between the college and the larger world. "There is," he says, "a parochialism that seems to penetrate many higher learning institutions, an intellectual and social isolation that reduces the effectiveness of the college and limits the vision of the student. We feel compelled to ask: How can the undergraduate college help students gain perspective and prepare them to meet their civic and social obligations in the neighborhood, the nation, and the world?"[28] In recent years the highly specialized character of many university disciplines, with their arcane vocabulary, methods of inquiry, and autonomous subject matter, has inevitably aggravated this situation.

It is student experience of this isolation that in large measure lay behind their shrill demands for relevance in the 1960s and 1970s and that we see reflected today in that apathy toward learning that so troubles concerned faculty. The third world is not unaware of this apathy and isolation, and frequently indicts American colleges and universities for estranging their students as a privileged caste without any sense of international solidarity. In a study of this phenomenon several years ago, Michael Buckley recalled that it was such alienation between educated taste and human sensibility which stunned Dorothy Thompson just after the Second World War when she visited Dachau and found in the SS quarters the poetry of Goethe and the music of Beethoven next to windows opening out to the execution ranges and the ovens. She concluded that the best of higher education was capable of producing people with cultivated skills, interests, and tastes but isolated from their own humanity, with little sensitivity to the burdens of their fellow human beings.[29]

The challenge for educators, then, according to Buckley, is to recognize in and through their disciplines that the twentieth century has produced something new in human awareness, namely a sense of the human person and the human community as such, of global interdependence, of the forces that bind all peoples together, of our common struggles to survive and grow as a species on planet earth. To be responsive to all that hinders such survival and growth, to human pain, privation, exploitation and injustice, must therefore become part of what it means to be human and educated in our time. By the same token, any insensitivity and indifference to such struggles must mark a person finally as uneducated, no matter how sharp the mind or cultivated the taste. Educators have to be convinced that students graduating from college today without this awareness of human solidarity are somehow diminished, their education failing to put them in touch with the mass of humankind.

How precisely to accomplish this educational goal of citizenship in the global village is no easy matter. Historically disciplines have not been geared to awakening student sensitivities to social injustice and human exploitation. There will ordinarily be few occasions for students to learn about the "absolute poor," for example, peoples so limited by malnutrition, illiteracy, disease, high infant mortality and low life expectancy as to be below the standards for a decent human life. The fact that no one seems to know how many humans are in this condition is itself significant (the most conservative estimate is 100 million, with third world population now doubling every thirty-five years). Nor will students routinely hear in their classes about the widespread poverty and homelessness here in the United States, or about the brutalities of our penal system, or the ravages to human dignity caused by unemployment, or the millions of old people hidden away in cheap rooms or exploited in nursing homes. Yet to care about any one of these societal problems, to be truly disturbed by the glaring contrast between the opulent life possible in industrialized nations and the despair blanketing half the globe, is to achieve a true goal of liberal education in the twentieth century.

A Carnegie Foundation Report in 1981 issued this warning:

> Today many Americans are shockingly ill-informed about public issues.... As a nation we are becoming civically illiterate. Unless we find better ways to educate ourselves *as citizens*, we run the risk of drifting unwittingly into a new kind of Dark Age — a time when small cadres of specialists will control knowledge, and thus control the decision-making process.... Schools and colleges simply must help students understand the process by which public policy is shaped, and prepare them to make informed discriminating judgments on questions that will affect the nation's future.[30]

The task of higher education is thus not simply to awaken student sensitivities to widespread human need, but also to foster "informed discriminating judgments" of such need; not simple description but critical analysis.

Critical analysis is so needed because no human situation just happens: each has its own roots and causes, historical, sociological, scientific, psychological, religious, economic, philosophical, ideological. Insofar as college students become sensitive to any such situation, they will naturally be drawn to ask the "why" questions they are supposed to ask, but they will ask these now from the viewpoint of the downtrodden, and the answers they hear will not be answers to an intellectual problem only but to a human problem, of which they themselves already have some vicarious experience. Needless to say, educators who attempt such a rational analysis of the human condition will not have an easy time combining compassion and competence, critical intelligence and moral sensitivity. We need only look at the phenomenon of global hunger and the scandal of poverty here in America to realize why this is so.

Concern for the hungry people in the world, for example, must entail a recognition that there are no simple solutions to the food problem. Virtually all authorities agree that global hunger is due not primarily to overpopulation or lack of food availability, but to the maldistribution of income and to the human inability to cope with the complexities of food distribution. Overpopulation in underdeveloped countries is really a symptom of poverty, not its cause. Even when relief efforts are successful in affected areas and the population growth rate decreases, much of the hunger problem remains untouched because the people who need food most simply cannot afford to buy it. Food crises thus reflect the rules of the international economic game. Contrary to popular belief, giant companies operating in poor countries often tend to displace more workers than they create jobs for, hence swelling the ranks of the unemployed and exercising a negative influence on income distribution. On the other hand, without such outside investment, it is extremely difficult for a poor country to develop any purchasing power of its own. It is to the advantage of the great food conglomerates, moreover, and to the American balance of trade generally, to export grain to these developing countries, thus inhibiting increase in their own food production. Yet many of these same countries also hurt themselves by pushing export crops, such as coffee and sugar, at the expense of food staples for their own people.[31]

Seeking to understand the scandal of poverty in the richest country on earth is an even more difficult undertaking in higher education. Indeed, the truly poor seem to be a cause of acute embarrassment to middle America and I suspect to the average college student also. In a nation where the middle-class dream has been promoted by government, industry, media, advertising, and churches, reports of abject poverty are unwelcome reminders that something is radically wrong in the land. In her magisterial study *The Idea of Poverty*, Gertrude Himmelfarb chronicles the utter astonishment that greeted the publication in 1861 of Henry Mayhew's authoritative report on "the undiscovered country" of the London poor, about whom he said less was known than "the most distant tribes on the earth." The facts he adduced were, reviewers kept saying, "tales stranger than fiction."[32] Through her detailed presentation of political, economic, and literary history, Himmelfarb traces the movement of poverty conceived as a natural calamity to poverty understood and accepted as a separate culture of social inequality, requiring the "services" of the modern welfare state. It is such acceptance of poverty without indignation that constitutes the problem for civilized society today.

The Census Bureau in Washington gives us what is probably the best indicator of the extent of poverty in the United States. In November 1987 the bureau announced that 14 percent of all Americans, over 33.1 million people, were living below the poverty line.[33] These figures count only cash income. The bureau also measures the number by including in a complex set of calculations the full market value of noncash benefits, such as food stamps, school lunches, medical care, and public housing subsidies. According to this more complex measure somewhere between 21.5 and 30.4 million were living in poverty. Most of these poor were white, 69 percent, and most of them had jobs, 41.5 percent of those over age fourteen. The "working poor" were in fact the fastest growing segment of the population, 8.9 million in 1986 compared to 6.5 million in 1979. Children were the poorest age group: 20.5 percent of all American children and almost 25 percent of those under age six were living below the poverty line.[34]

What, students ought to be asking themselves, is society to do about all these people? The traditional liberal response has been for better "services" to compensate for such social disadvantages, while conservatives believe that overly generous liberal programs create a "welfare mentality" that erodes initiative and personal responsibility.[35] Educators must help students think critically about these conflicting political, social, and economic analyses. Are they aware, for instance, that shortages of jobs is only one of the causes of poverty, that almost 70 percent of those below the poverty line simply cannot work at all, either because they are too old, or too disabled, or mothers of small children with no child-care, or themselves under fourteen years of age? Are we to relegate these millions to an "underclass," outside the labor force altogether, nonemployed rather than unemployed? And what is to be said of the "feminization of poverty," the fact that families headed by women — divorced, separated, widowed, deserted, and single — constitute the fastest growing portion of the poverty population?[36]

While the risk of elitism in American higher education is serious and unavoidable, it can be minimized to a great extent if educators acknowledge its presence and seek to counteract it within themselves and their disciplines. I think that much the same can be said for the second risk, that of value neutrality. In *The Aims of Education* Whitehead insists that there is a threefold rhythm in all intellectual growth, moving from the stage of romance or first apprehension, through the stage of disciplined precision to the final stage of generalization and synthesis. While these stages represent successive levels of involvement and understanding, they also constitute three simultaneous emphases, one or other of which may dominate as the rhythm changes.[37] Literature and art, for example, can provide insight into human experiences in the first stage, but these experiences must also be subjected in the second stage to the colder scrutiny of the natural and social sciences. However, before students can discern any moral imperatives for their own lives, they must move on to the larger questions of the third stage, involving the ultimate foundation, value, and direction of human life. It is in this third stage of the college curriculum that some provision must be made for weighing the data of experience by traditional moral and ethical standards.

In large measure this weighing will be conditioned by the mindset of students, their perception of reality. The North American mindset has been variously characterized as "thing-focused," "success-oriented," as "fascinated by technique and what works." Our bias is toward efficiency, competition, and quantitative results. We ask "how" questions much more easily than "why" questions of meaning and purpose. All these elements in our mindset result in social institutions and social structures that are products and projections of our internal attitudes and unquestioned values. Studies have shown, for example, that there has been a steady relaxation of traditional definitions of work, marriage, parenthood, and self in the American public, a personal liberation of mores that runs counter to the apparent growth in political conservatism. College students have thus been moving away from socially integrated paradigms and have been structuring their lives around paradigms that are much more personalized.[38]

The educational question, therefore, is whether universities can get students to scrutinize this shift taking place in their lives from community values to highly individualistic values, as well as their general inclination to focus on the private, the familial, the idiosyncratic, the here and now. They ought to be made aware, first of all, that this kind of shift is not at all new in American life. The period before World War I, the depression years before World War II, the late 1950s through the 1960s, all these progressive eras were characterized by a communal sense, by an emphasis upon duty to others, responsibility, and the importance of giving. One has only to think of how generally supportive most Americans were in the 1950s and 1960s of those efforts of blacks to overcome racial segregation and economic discrimination. These times offered a sense of movement, excitement, and adventure. Their theme was promise and their leaders charismatic. But these eras have all been followed by periods of disillusionment, when people simply got tired of doing and giving, especially giving their lives in war. They wanted more satisfaction and less asceticism, were more pragmatic, concerned with their rights rather than with their responsibilities, more interested in themselves than in others. We live now in one of these periods.

The affluence of our culture following World War II conditioned us as a nation to expanded choice and immediate self-fulfillment, experiences that are now being contradicted by the realities of economic limitation. The economic restlessness has engendered psychological restlessness. It seems quite normal today for people to draw into themselves in an effort to create small corners of rationality. Some still carry on the radical commitment to justice which flourished in the 1960s, but they are no longer the role models for youth. Sensitivity to civil rights and women's rights, opposition to apartheid in South Africa and oppression in Central America, promotion of equality of opportunity for all, these must be seen as the exception today, not the rule. College students may have just as much capacity for generosity, friendship, and concern for those in need as always, but the times neither encourage nor challenge these traits. They are there and can still be tapped, but not unless both faculty and students make some conscious effort to do so.

The risk today, then, is not that students will abandon a moral point of view in their personal lives, but that they will simply respond with inertia when challenged to reflect upon morally responsible behavior in the public sphere. Without such reflection, however, they will proceed to act in this arena after graduation not so much on the wrong moral principles as on no moral principles. In 1988 the thirty-three member Commission on National Challenges to Higher Education wrote a *Memorandum to the 41st President*, which they distributed to all presidential candidates that year. One of the five acute deficiencies to be alleviated, they said, was loss of respect for fundamental values and ethical behavior in government and business. Alluding to widely publicized scandals in both areas, they emphasized that because "nearly every future politician, businessman, physician, lawyer, teacher, journalist and clergyman will attend colleges and universities," these institutions must put students in touch with standards of public behavior "through offering traditional courses on philosophy, religion, literature, history and political science as well as newer courses specifically directed to moral reasoning and professional ethics."[39]

This can be an embarrassing recommendation for many educators who, because they are not professional ethicists, have traditionally felt absolved from dealing with the ethical aspects of their discipline. Yet, to cite just two examples, all economic behavior and all political life have their moral dimensions, from which economics and political science can detach themselves as disciplines only at high cost to the student. Students cannot make moral decisions if they are not taught what moral decisions there are to be made. The business world has learned to its sorrow that it is not easy to assume moral viewpoints on business transactions that one has been trained to deal with from viewpoints divorced from morality. Harold S. Geneen, Chief Executive Officer of International Telephone and Telegraph Corporation for seventeen years and not without critics of his own business integrity, once said that "among the board of directors of Fortune 500 companies I estimate that 95 percent are not doing what they are legally, morally and ethically supposed to do." Failure of managerial trust, moreover, is generally acknowledged to be even more pervasive than incidents reported in the press and to involve what is really a system-wide corruption supported by organizational norms.[40]

The sudden emergence in American colleges of whole clusters of courses in ethics — business ethics, ethics of peace and war, legal ethics, medical ethics — testifies to the seriousness of efforts to push student reflection on values and value commitment out into the wider communities in which they will spend their lives. But educators have to remember that these are not the students of a decade or two ago. The 1987 annual survey of freshmen by the Higher Education Research Institute found that material wealth and career success continue to be a central concern: 75.6 percent of freshmen polled said that "being very well off financially" was one of their top personal goals, compared to 39.1 percent who said this in 1970. At the same time, the percentage who called "developing a meaningful philosophy of life" an important goal dropped to 39.4 percent, down from 82.9 percent in 1967.[41] Hence it should come as no surprise that students with such mindsets have little interest in coming to terms with problems of conscience in society. It is much easier for them to think of leadership in their future careers as coming from mere information and expertise rather than from wisdom, value commitment, and sensitivity to community needs. If we are to believe the social research of Daniel Yankelovich, there is yet another burden on educators: to find new ways to combine the teleology and stability that characterized traditional ethics with the compulsion of students to focus on immediate personal growth and freedom of choice. He documents at great length the rejection in the prosperous 1950s and 1960s of the old American ethos of self-denial, and the current disillusionment, amid the belt-tightening of the 1980s, with the ethos of self-fulfillment that took its place. Because as a nation we are now trying slowly to understand a new economic order, we inevitably face an extended period of social and psychological restlessness. People, says Yankelovich, especially the young, are beginning to feel weakened without community: "its absence is experienced as an aching loss, a void" that results in "feelings of isolation, falseness, instability and impoverishment of spirit." It is this experience that is gradually coming to mediate between narrow self-interests and desires for greater connectedness with the world. "So," his long study concludes, "we now need a new social ethic.... We need new rules to define the epochal tasks that must be accomplished in our era to bring about that minimal harmony between individual and society that is the mark of a successful civilization."[42]

4. Law, Religion, and Prism Focus

Yankelovich's cautious optimism that private and public concerns will gradually begin to merge in students' minds is a vote of confidence that American liberal education will not in the end become the victim of either elitism or value neutrality. Robert Bellah and his collaborators, though perhaps more cautious even than Yankelovich, have uncovered signs that as a society we may be retrieving somewhat our biblical and republican traditions.

These traditions are so important because their languages may eventually enable us to recognize more easily that human happiness and self-fulfillment must also include involvement in civic life and relationships to others in community. Cultures, says Bellah, are dramatic conversations about things that matter to their participants, and what is beginning to matter to Americans is discovering some antidote to their fragmented lives, some hope for a just and compassionate society, some sense of the common good.[43] If this is the culture into which higher education is initiating its students, then both educators and educated must necessarily become participants in this tentative sociological shift.

The world of the American college and university is thus inching its way ever so slowly in the same direction as the world of American law and religion. Were we able to graph this movement, we should see how the lines of these three institutions hesitatingly converge, overlap, and converge again at the various points where each becomes most sensitive to the common good. We have taken note of several of these intersections already. It remains now to indicate briefly the more important ways that law and religion can influence this directional change. To return to our image of the prism: how we focus this body of glass determines how we see the light it disperses. In the educational experience law and religion act precisely as agents of perception, able either to sharpen or to dull education's focus, and thus to determine how students absorb the knowledge dispersed.

The fundamental fact, never to be lost sight of in speaking of the common good, is that as a people we Americans have always been much more disposed toward individualism than toward community. This disposition is endemic, shot through our culture, going back to the insistent demand for religious freedom in colonial times. The observation of Edmund Burke has often been quoted: the colonists' religion, he said, represented "a refinement on the principle of resistance: it is the dissidence of dissent, and the protestantism of the Protestant religion."[44] Virulent forms of sectarianism, such as the Baptists and other dissenters, found willing allies in Jefferson and the "enlightened," who wanted this same freedom in order to fragment the sects and neutralize their political influence. In both cases religious liberty was understood as the absence of all compulsion by government, which by implication was seen by many sectarians to be essentially coercive in character. The more benign republican tradition, especially in its pure form, emphasized the need for a community of citizens obligated mutually and responsibly to seek the public good of all. Though permanently lodged in our political life as an ideal, these moral requirements of republicanism have never been dominant in our culture as a whole. Subordinating one's personal or group interest to public interest has simply not been an attractive option for the American mind.

Now it matters very much for the outcome of one's education — that is to say, for how one functions in society — whether one thinks of law and government as mainly coercive, to be used either as threat or protection, or whether one thinks of them rather as instruments for promoting a shared societal purpose. In the latter case community is conceived as compatible with pluralism — religious, moral, economic, or social — whereas in the former case the two are presumed to be opposites. If one's thinking follows a republican model, then social asymmetry is able to be reconciled with egalitarianism through the concept of membership, and thus tends both to neutralize questions of external authority and control and to limit the scope of law. As soon as one begins to think of diverse social groups simply as "others," however, the scope of law is immediately widened and one begins to doubt that society can ever be both egalitarian and ordered. Law is then seen primarily as protector of one's individuality, and the collective as a threat to human dignity and enterprise.[45]

Because students usually believe deeply in their individuality, they will generally become more vulnerable to elitism insofar as they are convinced that concern for the common good means an erosion of their legitimate self-interest. Discussions of social justice will then tend to make them uncomfortable and defensive, especially if these discussions focus on the plight of the poor. Hence it is important for them to realize that even though law gives the appearance of objectivity in the pursuit of justice, it is too often administered for the benefit of those who have power to enforce it. When the poor resort to some crude manifestation of force, therefore, it is usually because they have lost confidence that the law will be administered fairly in their behalf. They are much less concerned with limiting someone else's self-interest than with protecting their own, and they have learned from bitter experience that public bureaucracies yield only to public pressure.

Thus it is extremely important that students come to appreciate the positive role of law in society and not become cynical about the common good because law and the legal processes are frequently held captive by vested interests. For law always stands at the crucial point of policy and at its best can succeed in mediating the influence of public ideals and values on the practical programs of social institutions. Nowhere is this more evident today than in education itself. At the end of 1987 the League of Women Voters conducted a poll of its members to find out the topics they most wanted presidential candidates to debate. Education had more of their support than health care, arms control, and defense combined.[46] Surely this was because these members saw that the education reform they wanted was so difficult to achieve, requiring the cooperation of federal, state, and local authorities in a political context in which the pursuit of particular interests is never possible apart from a recognition and acceptance of the general community interest.

Just as the risk of elitism can be reduced or heightened by how one believes law should operate in society, so an undergraduate's commitment to values can be conditioned by how she or he is influenced by religion. To put this influence in context, we should recognize that while all Americans have firm commitments to broad cultural values, such as freedom, independence, equality, and self-government, it is not easy at any given time to determine what patterns of social relationships or organizational structures are meaningful expressions of these values. For what determines the texture of contemporary life are not values as such, but the ways they are given life in social institutions. Because these are constantly changing, value conflict is inevitable. Moreover, just as it is difficult to conceptualize values apart from their institutional form, so it is also difficult to separate them from the vested interests with which they are usually associated. While these interests may often be quite legitimate, the educated person must be able to isolate them if he or she is to avoid becoming their captive. Insofar as a given religious tradition is sensitive to the common good, therefore, it can help to facilitate this task.

While the study of religion has always been central to the liberal education of undergraduates in church-related schools, for many years such study was relegated to an academic limbo in most secular institutions in America. Today this has changed. Like the revival of religion in the various sectors of society during the last decade or so, there has been a serious renewal of interest in religious experience on the part of scholars in almost every academic discipline. The questions they ask center on how religion operates in society and how it affects the human development of persons, and the answers they give are usually in terms of value critique and commitment, however diverse and pluralist these values and their religious roots may be. Hence there is usually ample opportunity for students, sensitized during their college years to the demands of human dignity and equality, to learn what the various religious traditions have to say about the common good of their society.

In *Protestant-Catholic-Jew*, his classic study of a generation ago, sociologist Will Herberg argued that, as immigrants became assimilated into American life, the third generation looked for ways to reestablish its distinctive identity. For many, religion was used to fulfill that need. It thereby became, not a source of prophetic witness, but the basis for one's specific identity as an American. The result, Herberg said, was that the religious and moral perspectives of large numbers in the nation during the 1950s were interpenetrated with their whole experience of the American way of life. They desperately wanted religion to legitimate their vested economic and political interests, because these had always been perceived as part of the *religious* meaning of their lives.[47] The problem today, however, is that, with religious institutions becoming more conscious of the common good, they are exercising a much more prophetic function in society and no longer providing the traditional plausibility structure for dominant social institutions. The outlook of undergraduates cannot but be affected by this shift.

Capitalism is one such institution that has recently come under criticism from the churches, because the wealth it produces is so unequally distributed and the extent of poverty in America so great. Many feel that business is being given a bad name by this criticism. And yet, when religious belief in a transcendent God addresses any political or economic or social system, we should expect the ideals and aspirations of that religion to stand in constant critical judgment, reminding its members of the standards by which their current practices, as well as those of the nation, are ever being weighed and found wanting. To be committed to religious values is surely not to be committed to one's nation as it is, but rather to the just secular society, in which the equal dignity of all persons is recognized, as well as their right to a share in goods and services corresponding to their basic human needs. This is what has always been understood as the common good, something which is gradually coming to be seen in religious circles as the norm for judging the health of America, as well as how best to limit the greed and avarice inevitably encouraged by a capitalist economy.[48]

I do not wish to suggest that religion's major role in the education of the young is to give them a message about society. Religion's message has always been and must always be one about God. But since God is profoundly and personally related to us in all that is fully human, there is no separate and sacred realm where God is to be found. In other words, from a religious point of view there is no such thing as an autonomous man or woman with God as object, and never has been. What religion asserts about the secular educational process is that within it the creative and redemptive action of God is continually operative. Indeed, it is practically impossible to distinguish in that process the salvific from the merely human. If students go deep enough into this human, therefore, they will find not only their true selves but God. By the same token, whatever relationship they have with God must come from and through their human experiences here and now. The educational task is thus to enable them to embrace these experiences with insight and intellectual freedom, and to develop a sense of God sufficiently great that it does not depend on those limited religious horizons which so often crumble under the impact of intellectual challenge.

Let me close with two final observations. First, colleges and universities are not the moral watchdogs of society. They are not infallible either in what faculty believe or in what students are taught. They are not places to go for indoctrination, whether political, social, economic, or religious, nor do they have any obligation to tell society how to act. But they do have an obligation to their students, to help them to become reflective and compassionate, capable of grasping society's problems and conflicting ideologies, willing to make critical judgments on the world's values and the direction they believe it should take in the future. They desperately need sensitivity to the human condition and to have that sensitivity refined by intellectual analysis and precision. Above all they need to understand the power of moral conviction and the often high cost of making a wise and ethical choice.

Second, we cannot expect that colleges and universities, in seeking to fulfill their obligation to students, can ever be disconnected from the culture around them, for their task is precisely to prepare citizens to function at a mature level in that culture. Hence we should not be surprised when these institutions reflect whatever turmoil is present in national life as a whole. Just now this is at a dramatic high: economic, sociological, demographic, and technological change is to be seen everywhere in America. If institutions as relatively stable and conservative as law and religion are feeling the effects, higher education cannot but feel them too. Its disarray in curriculum and confusion in goals is simply a mirror of the disarray and confusion in the culture generally. We must indeed continue to criticize both curriculum and goals, but nostalgia for a more ordered past will never give us resources to face the future, either in education or in anything else; it will only lead to despondency and fear. Our hope must be found in the present, in our hesitant public efforts at conversation about the things that matter, in our ever-present national commitment to unity, and in the caution with which we venture to affirm those values and ideals that still divide us.

NOTES

Preface

1. *Abington School District* v. *Schempp*, 374 U.S. 203, 231 (1963). Brennan's comment is from his long concurring opinion in this case.
2. *Tilton* v. *Richardson*, 403 U.S. 672, 678 (1971).
3. From an address by Justice Brennan at Georgetown University, October 12, 1985, reported in the *New York Times*, October 13, 1985.
4. On the conservative side see Alasdair MacIntyre, *After Virtue* (Notre Dame, Ind.: University of Notre Dame Press, 1981); on the liberal side see Bruce A. Ackerman, *Social Justice and the Liberal State* (New Haven: Yale University Press, 1980).
5. Edward Gibbon, *The Decline and Fall of the Roman Empire*, chapter 2, section 1 (New York: Modern Library edition, vol. 1, 1932), 25–26.
6. The original version of Part I appeared in the September 1987 issue of *Second Opinion*; sections of Part II in *Politics and Religion*, edited by W. Lawson Taitte, published by the University of Texas Press.

Part I. Finding the Cultural Matrix

1. *Zorach* v. *Clauson*, 343 U.S. 306, 313.
2. H. Richard Niebuhr, *Christ and Culture* (New York: Harper & Row Torchbooks, 1956), 32–39.
3. Daniel Yankelovich, *New Rules, Searching for Self-Fulfillment in a World Turned Upside Down* (New York: Random House, 1981), xiii–xiv. See comments of Lynn Buzzard, "America

Today: Shaking Foundations," in Lynn Buzzard, ed., *Freedom and Faith* (Westchester, Ill.: Crossway Books, 1982), 11–20.

4. Everett Carll Ladd, "Secular and Religious America," in Richard John Neuhaus, ed., *Unsecular America* (Grand Rapids, Mich.: Eerdmans, 1986), 24–25. Peter L. Berger discusses at length the loss of religious domination in dealing with the phenomenon in *The Sacred Canopy* (New York: Doubleday Anchor Books, 1969), 105–125.

5. Harold J. Berman, *The Interaction of Law and Religion* (Nashville: Abingdon Press, 1974), 64–65.

6. See Ladd, "Secular and Religious America," 26–27.

7. Oliver Wendell Holmes, Jr., "The Path of the Law," *Harvard Law Review* 10 (1897), 461; Holmes, *The Common Law* (Cambridge, Mass.: Harvard University Press, 1963), 5.

8. The legal historian most responsible for this understanding of law is James Willard Hurst. See especially *The Growth of American Law: The Lawmakers* (Boston: Little, Brown, 1950) and *Law and Social Order in the United States* (Ithaca, N.Y.: Cornell University Press, 1977).

9. Christopher F. Mooney, *Public Virtue: Law and the Social Character of Religion* (Notre Dame, Ind.: University of Notre Dame Press, 1986), 80–92.

10. Jerold S. Auerbach, *Unequal Justice* (New York: Oxford University Press, 1976), 9.

11. See Roberto Mangabeira Unger, *The Critical Legal Studies Movement* (Cambridge, Mass.: Harvard University Press, 1986); David Kairys, ed., *The Politics of Law* (New York: Pantheon, 1982).

12. William K. Muir, Jr., *Law and Attitude Change* (Chicago: University of Chicago Press, 1973), 138.

13. Lawrence M. Friedman, *American Law* (New York: W. W. Norton, 1984), 278, 256.

14. See Robert A. Vraciu, "Hospital Strategies of the Eighties: A Mid-Decade Look," *HCM Review*, Fall 1985, 12–15.

15. Lawrence M. Friedman, *A History of American Law*, 2nd ed. (New York: Simon & Schuster, 1985), 662.

16. Mooney, *Public Virtue*, 21–28.

17. Elwyn A. Smith, "Voluntary Establishment of Religion," in Elwyn A. Smith, ed., *The Religion of the Republic* (Philadelphia: Fortress Press, 1971), 154–182.

18. Dissonance phenomena were first researched by Leon Festinger, *A Theory of Cognitive Dissonance* (Stanford: Stanford University Press, 1957). The theory has been applied to religious choice by Peter L. Berger in *The Heretical Imperative* (New York: Doubleday Anchor Books, 1979).

19. Martin E. Marty, *The Search for a Usable Future* (New York: Harper & Row, 1969), 68–72.

20. Thomas Luckmann, *The Invisible Religion: The Problem of Religion in Modern Society* (New York: Macmillan, 1967). See the comments of Martin E. Marty, "Religion in America since Mid-century," *Daedalus*, Winter 1982, 154–157.

21. On secular and theistic humanism, see the extended treatment by A. James Reichley, *Religion in American Public Life* (Washington: The Brookings Institution, 1985), 41–52, 344–350. See also George M. Marsden, "Are Secularists the Threat? Is Religion the Solution?" in Richard John Neuhaus, *Unsecular America*, 31–45.

22. As far as anyone knows, the term *secular humanism* originated in an *amicus curiae* brief to the Supreme Court from the American Humanist Association in *Torcaso v. Watkins*, 367 U.S. 488 (1961). Roy Torcaso, an atheist and an appointee to the office of notary public in Maryland, was barred from office by a provision of the state constitution because he would not declare his belief in God. A unanimous Court said that goverment cannot aid religions based on belief in the existence of God as against those founded on different beliefs. In a footnote Justice Black added: "Among religions in this country which do not teach what would generally be considered belief in God are Buddhism, Taoism, Ethical Culture, Secular Humanism and others." See the discussion on the op. ed. page of the *New York Times* for June 2 and 19, 1985.

23. *New York Times*, February 22, 1985. With current emphasis on holding down government spending, no money is likely to be appropriated for the program to create magnet schools in cities that are desegregating. So the issue of what cannot be taught as "secular humanism" is never likely to be clarified.

24. See, on the Protestant side, George A. Lindbeck, *The Nature of Doctrine* (Philadelphia: Westminster Press, 1984); John Howard Yoder, *The Politics of Jesus* (Grand Rapids, Mich.: Eerdmans, 1972); Stanley Hauerwas, *The Peaceable Kingdom*

(Notre Dame, Ind.: University of Notre Dame Press, 1983). On the Catholic side the most authoritative statement is that of Joseph Ratzinger, *The Ratzinger Report* (San Francisco: Ignatius Press, 1985). The Vatican statement censuring Küng appeared in the *New York Times*, December 19, 1979; the statement censuring Curran appeared in the *National Catholic Reporter*, March 21, 1986.

25. Robert N. Bellah et al., *Habits of the Heart* (Berkeley: University of California Press, 1985).

26. Wade Clark Roof, "America's Voluntary Establishment: Mainline Religion in Transition," *Daedalus*, Winter 1982, 165–184.

27. Berger, *Sacred Canopy*, 111–112.

28. Niebuhr, *Christ and Culture*, 187–188.

29. See Robin W. Lovin, ed., *Religion and American Public Life* (New York: Paulist Press, 1986), for several different approaches to the prophetic tradition.

30. Historically this theological emphasis is much more characteristic of the Catholic than of the Protestant tradition, but in recent years it has appeared more strongly in both traditions, cutting across liberals and conservatives. See, for example, John B. Cobb, Jr., *Process Theology as Political Theology* (Philadelphia: Westminster Press, 1982); J. Philip Wogaman, *Economics and Ethics* (Philadelphia: Fortress Press, 1986); Michael Novak, *Will It Liberate?* (New York: Paulist Press, 1986); Johannes B. Metz, *Theology of the World* (New York: Herder & Herder, 1969); John A. Coleman, *An American Strategic Theology* (New York: Paulist Press, 1982).

31. Edmond Cahn, *The Moral Decision* (Bloomington: Indiana University Press, 1981), 35.

32. Harold J. Berman, "The Interaction of Law and Religion," *Mercer Law Review* 31 (1980), 411.

33. Karl Llewellyn, *The Bramble Bush* (Dobbs Ferry, N.Y.: Oceana Publications, 1960), 145.

34. Friedman, *History*, 674–678, gives an overview of law reform.

35. See, for example, David Luban, ed., *The Good Lawyer: Lawyers' Roles and Lawyers' Ethics* (Totowa, N.J.: Rowman & Allanheld, 1984).

36. Douglas Sturm, "Religious Sensibility and the Reconstruc-

tion of Public Life: Prospectus for a New America," in Lovin, *Religion*, 56.

37. This is the argument of Bellah, *Habits of the Heart*. See the incisive overview of this large question by David Hollenbach, "The Common Good Revisited." *Theological Studies* 50 (1989), 70–94.

38. For example, MacIntyre, *After Virtue*.

39. See the argument of Michael Walzer, *Spheres of Justice: A Defense of Pluralism and Equality* (New York: Basic Books, 1983).

40. Jeffrey Stout, "Liberal Society and the Language of Morals," *Soundings* 69 (1986), 53. See also Mark Silk, *Spiritual Politics: Religion and America Since World War II* (New York: Simon & Schuster, 1988).

41. See Yankelovich, *New Rules*, 249.

42. Alexis de Tocqueville, *Democracy in America*, trans. George Lawrence, ed. J. P. Mayer (New York: Doubleday Anchor Books, 1969), 292.

43. Robin W. Lovin, "Religion and American Public Life: Three Relationships," in Lovin, *Religion*, 26.

44. MacIntyre, *After Virtue*, 236.

45. Lovin, *Religion*, 24.

46. Kent Greenawalt, *Religious Convictions and Public Choice* (New York: Oxford University Press, 1987), 231. See especially pp. 215–230.

47. For example, Richard John Neuhaus, *The Naked Public Square* (Grand Rapids, Mich.: Eerdmans, 1984).

48. Mona Harrington, *The Dream of Deliverance in American Politics* (New York: Knopf, 1986), 16.

49. Reinhold Niebuhr, *Moral Man and Immoral Society* (New York: Scribner's, 1932), 3–4, 233.

50. Reinhold Niebuhr, *The Nature and Destiny of Man*, vol. 2 (New York: Scribner's, 1943), 85. See here the interpretation of Niebuhr by Robert McAfee Brown in his introduction to a collection of Niebuhr essays, *The Essential Reinhold Niebuhr* (New Haven, Conn.: Yale University Press, 1986), xi.

Part II: The Riddle of the Establishment Clause

1. For the Meese address and reactions, see articles in the *New York Times* for July 10, 1985, October 13, 1985, Octo-

ber 26, 1985, and June 12, 1986. Justice Brennan spoke at Georgetown University; Justice Stevens spoke at a Federal Bar Association meeting in Chicago: Justice White was dissenting in *Thornburgh* v. *American College of Obstetricians*, 476 U.S. 747, 789 (1986).

2. Even more accurate, though more cumbersome, would be to speak of the "interrelationship of the civil and religious communities." This phrasing would speak to the multitude of concrete churches as well as to the dispersal of governmental power in this country among the federal and state governments and local communities. It would also avoid the picture of two competing power structures with a clear line marking their separate functions. See Paul G. Kauper, *Religion and the Constitution* (Baton Rouge: Louisiana State University Press, 1964), 3–4; Richard P. McBrien, *Caesar's Coin* (New York: Macmillan, 1987), 24–26; John T. Noonan, Jr., *The Believer and the Powers That Are* (New York: Macmillan, 1987), xvi.

3. Bernard Bailyn, *The Ideological Origins of the American Revolution* (Cambridge, Mass.: Harvard University Press, 1967), ix.

4. Quoted by Henry F. May, *The Enlightenment in America* (New York: Oxford University Press, 1976), 100. May adds that one of the faults of the Enlightenment was "the belief that *everything* can be settled by compromise." See the discussion of the slavery question in Bailyn, *Ideological Origins* 234–246.

5. Bailyn, 271.

6. The act, originally called "A Bill" when drafted by Jefferson, is to be found in Merrill D. Peterson, ed., *The Portable Thomas Jefferson* (New York: Vintage Press, 1975), 251–253.

7. The Memorial is to be found in Robert S. Alley, ed., *James Madison on Religious Liberty* (Buffalo: Prometheus Books, 1985), 55–60. See Ralph L. Ketcham, "James Madison and Religion—A New Hypothesis," in ibid., 175–196.

8. Letter of January 22, 1786, in ibid., 62.

9. Letter of 1832 to Rev. Jasper Adams, in Gaillard Hunt, ed., *The Writings of James Madison*, vol. 9 (New York: G. P. Putnam's Sons, 1904), 487. Cited by Donald L. Drakeman, "Religion and the Republic: James Madison and the First Amendment," in Alley, *James Madison*, 238. Madison's second thoughts

will be found in his "Detached Memoranda," written between 1817 and 1832, in Alley, 89-94.

10. An early biographer of Madison, William C. Rives, reported that he was accustomed to quote "with great approbation" a remark of Voltaire's that he found in a book Jefferson sent him from Paris: "If one religion only were allowed in England, the government would possibly become arbitrary; if there were but two, the people would cut each others' throats; but, as there are such a multitude, they all live happy and in peace." See Ketcham, "James Madison and Religion," 191-192.

11. William Lee Miller, *The First Liberty* (New York: Knopf, 1986), 112-113. Miller's book is one of the most thorough and intelligent discussions of religion and the Constitution, and surely the most urbane. The interpretation here of *Federalist Papers* Nos. 10 and 51 is the one generally accepted today and is to be found in Gary Wills, *Explaining America: The Federalist* (New York: Doubleday, 1981), 97-264. See also Gordon S. Wood's extensive treatment in *The Creation of the American Republic* (Chapel Hill: University of North Carolina Press, 1969).

12. It seems clear today that Federalist theory was erroneous. Even though not contemplated at the time, the power to tax and spend for the general welfare might conceivably have been used to authorize support for religion. In his exhaustive but very biased study, *The Establishment Clause: Religion and the First Amendment* (New York: Macmillan, 1986), Leonard W. Levy recognizes (pp. 172-174) a long list of federal powers that could be used to aid religion, and in fact were used by the First Congress, as we shall see. It is puzzling, therefore, to find him arguing earlier (pp. 109-117 and elsewhere) that the federal government had no power at all to aid religion, and that no one thought the establishment clause created such power. Surely the issue is not what power the clause creates but the extent of its limitation on various powers already presumed to be in the Constitution. See the critique of Levy's book by Douglas Laycock in the *Journal of Law and Religion* 4 (1986), 241-251.

13. The texts are from the *Annals of the Congress of the United States*, compiled by Joseph Gales in 1834, cited by Michael J. Malbin, *Religion and Politics: The Intentions of the Authors of the First Amendment* (Washington: American Enterprise In-

stitute, 1978), 6–14. See also Drakeman, "Religion and the Republic," 233–234.

14. Arguing for this view are Leonard Levy, *The Establishment Clause*; Leo Pfeffer, *Religion, State and the Burger Court* (Buffalo: Prometheus Books, 1984); Thomas J. Curry, *The First Freedoms: Church and State in America to the Passage of the First Amendment* (New York: Oxford University Press, 1986).

15. This view is defended by Robert L. Cord, *Separation of Church and State: Historical Fact and Current Fiction* (New York: Lambeth Press, 1982); Walter Berns, *The First Amendment and the Future of American Democracy* (Chicago: Gateway Editions, 1985); Michael Malbin, *Religion and Politics*.

16. Berns, *The First Amendment*, 8.

17. See John Courtney Murray, *We Hold These Truths* (New York: Sheed & Ward, 1960), 48–63. For Murray, the disestablishment and free exercise provisions of the First Amendment, in their *objective* meaning and content, had to be considered as simply prudent lawmaking, "articles of peace," ways to keep public order in a pluralist society. The framers could not, he said, have intended to enact into civil law the theological or ideological convictions of any particular group (regarding freedom and authority) in such wise as to impose these on all Americans, for this would in effect have been to "establish" them as "articles of faith." Hence the *subjective* motivation of framers who might hold such convictions had to be irrelevant to the content of the amendment itself. Apparently Murray's fear was that basing the civil right of religious liberty on a theological understanding of freedom would have had the effect of legitimizing the autonomy of conscience and so of promoting religious indifferentism.

18. Drakeman, "Religion and the Republic," 235. See the sharp analysis of this whole question by Leonard W. Levy, *Original Intent and the Framers' Constitution* (New York: Macmillan, 1988).

19. Curry, *The First Freedoms*, 219. American religious historians have narrated in great detail how America became self-consciously Protestant in the course of the nineteenth century. See Robert T. Handy, *A Christian America: Protestant Hopes and Historical Realities* (New York: Oxford University Press, 2nd ed., 1984); Martin E. Marty, *Righteous Empire: The Protestant Experience in America* (New York: Dial Press, 1970); Sydney E.

Ahlstrom, *A Religious History of the American People* (New Haven: Yale University Press, 1972).

20. Joseph Story, *Commentaries on the Constitution of the United States*, 3 vols. (Boston: Gray Hilliard, 1833), 2:723-724. Quoted by John F. Wilson, "Common Religion in American Society," in Leroy S. Rouner, ed., *Civil Religion and Political Theology* (Notre Dame, Ind.: University of Notre Dame Press, 1986), 113-114.

21. Quoted by Robert T. Handy, "The Magna Charter of Religious Freedom in America," in John F. Wilson and Donald L. Drakeman, eds., *Church and State in American Society*, 2nd ed. (Boston: Beacon Press, 1987), 88-89.

22. Miller, *The First Liberty*, 234.

23. Handy, *A Christian America*, 87-90. See also Miller, *The First Liberty*, 261-262.

24. Daniel J. Boorstin, *The Americans* (New York: Random House, 1958), 19. For further development of this theme see Christopher F. Mooney, *Religion and the American Dream* (Philadelphia: Westminster Press, 1977).

25. See, among the many authors who have dealt with this phenomenon: Sidney E. Mead, *The Nation with the Soul of a Church* (New York: Harper & Row, 1975); Robert N. Bellah, *The Broken Covenant* (New York: Seabury Press, 1975); John F. Wilson, *Public Religion in American Culture* (Philadelphia: Temple University Press, 1979); Martin E. Marty, *The Public Church* (New York: Crossroad, 1981).

26. See Sidney E. Mead, *The Lively Experiment: The Shaping of Christianity in America* (New York: Harper & Row, 1963), 75ff; Mooney, *Religion and the American Dream*, 17-30.

27. Ahlstrom, *Religious History of the American People*, 879, 880.

28. See Mooney, *Public Virtue*, 6-11. See also the works by Wills, Wood, and Miller cited in note 11 *supra*.

29. Handy, *A Christian America*, 33-34.

30. In *The Lost Soul of American Politics* (New York: Basic Books, 1984) John Patrick Diggins dismisses the republican rhetoric of the Founders as historically insignificant. While they talked civic virtue, he argues, they enacted propertied interest. He apparently would not recognize that they actually said and did both. In any case, it does not seem very realistic to suppose

that their social reality could be cut off from their language, and the historical studies of Bailyn and Wood are persuasive arguments that it was not.

31. Ahlstrom, *Religious History of the American People*, 642.
32. De Tocqueville, *Democracy in America*, 448.
33. Ibid., 291–292.
34. Michael Walzer, *Obligations: Essays on Disobedience, War and Citizenship* (Cambridge, Mass.: Harvard University Press, 1970), 227.
35. De Tocqueville, *Democracy in America*, 515, 517.
36. *Davidson* v. *New Orleans*, 96 U.S. 97 (1878); *Hurtado* v. *California*, 110 U.S. 516 (1884).
37. *Lochner* v. *New York*, 198 U.S. 45 (1905), invalidated a New York law fixing the maximum number of working hours for bakers by holding that the right of employers to determine working hours constituted an economic "liberty" protected by the Fourteenth Amendment.
38. *Meyer* v. *Nebraska*, 262 U.S. 390, 399–400 (1923). See also from this period *Pierce* v. *Society of Sisters*, 268 U.S. 510 (1925).
39. Cord, *Separation of Church and State*, 99. I follow here Cord's history of the due process clause.
40. *Gitlow* v. *New York*, 268 U.S. 652, 666 (1925).
41. *DeJonge* v. *Oregon*, 299 U.S. 353, 364 (1937).
42. *Cantwell* v. *Connecticut*, 310 U.S. 296, 303–304 (1940).
43. As of now all but two of the procedural rights in the Bill of Rights have been held applicable to the states. The exceptions are the grand jury indictment requirement of the Fifth Amendment and the civil cases jury trial guarantee of the Seventh Amendment. First Amendment guarantees are the only substantive rights found so far to be "fundamental." The rarely litigated Second and Third Amendments, dealing with the substantive right to bear arms and with the quartering of soldiers, have never been incorporated.
44. Charles Fairman has concluded that there was clearly no intention to incorporate the Bill of Rights: "Does the Fourteenth Amendment Incorporate the Bill of Rights?" *Stanford Law Review* 2 (1949), 5–173; Michael Kent Curtis has concluded the exact opposite: *No State Shall Abridge* (Durham, N.C.: Duke University Press, 1986). In a celebrated dissent in 1947 Justice

Black argued strongly that the Bill of Rights as a whole had been incorporated in 1868: *Adamson* v. *California*, 332 U.S. 46, 68–123 (1947); his argument was never accepted by the Court, however, and was opposed especially by Justice Frankfurter both in *Adamson* and in later cases.

45. *Everson* v. *Board of Education*, 330 U.S. 1 (1947).

46. *West Virginia State Board of Education* v. *Barnette*, 319 U.S. 624 (1943). I follow here the insights of Mark de Wolfe Howe, *The Garden and the Wilderness* (Chicago: University of Chicago Press, 1965), 107–118.

47. I discuss these cases in *Public Virtue*, 36–54. The "play in the joints" phrase is former Chief Justice Warren Burger's in *Walz* v. *Tax Commission*, 397 U.S. 664, 669 (1970).

48. *McCollum* v. *Board of Education*, 333 U.S. 203, 216 (1948).

49. *Abington School District* v. *Schempp*, 374 U.S. 203, 254–258 (1963).

50. The phrase is that of Justice Benjamin Cardoza in *Palko* v. *Connecticut*, 302 U.S. 319, 325 (1937). See Kauper, *Religion and the Constitution*, 50–57.

51. *Abington School District* v. *Schempp*, 223, 217. It was in the *Schempp* case that the Supreme Court first elaborated its rule that what the establishment clause forbids is any state action whose purpose or primary effect is the advancement of religion, even when no danger to personal liberty can be demonstrated. A statement in Justice Brennan's concurring opinion is also instructive: "Even if we assume that the draftsmen of the Fourteenth Amendment saw no immediate connection between its protection against state action infringing personal liberty and the guarantees of the First Amendment, it is certainly too late in the day to suggest that their assumed inattention to this question dilutes the force of these constitutional guarantees in their application to the States." Ibid., 257.

52. See Howe, *The Garden and the Wilderness*, 133–143.

53. See Reichley, *Religion in American Public Life*, 135–167. For the item on state constitutions Reichley refers to Leo Pfeffer, *God, Caesar and the Constitution* (Boston: Beacon Press, 1975), 259.

54. *Buckley* v. *Valeo*, 424 U.S. 1, 291 (1976).

55. *Walz* v. *Tax Commission*, 669.

56. Will Herberg, *Protestant-Catholic-Jew* (New York: Doubleday Anchor Books, revised ed., 1960).
57. J. R. Pole, *The Pursuit of Equality in American History* (Berkeley: University of California Press, 1978), 325–326.
58. This poll of 1,254 respondents was reported in the *New York Times*, May 26, 1987.
59. Howe, *The Garden and the Wilderness*, 32.
60. See the overview of this defense in Mooney, *Public Virtue*, 28–36.
61. Howe, 151.
62. *Everson v. Board of Education*, 18. See the comments in Howe, 149–161.
63. *Zorach v. Clauson*, 343 U.S. 306, 320 (1952).
64. Howe, 157.
65. See Leo Pfeffer's argument in *Church, State and Freedom* (Boston: Beacon Press, 1953), 498–499.
66. *Abington School District v. Schempp*, 313.
67. See *McCollum v. Board of Education*, especially the concurring opinion of Justice Frankfurter, 333 U.S. 203, 216 (1948). See also Howe, 140–141.
68. *Zorach v. Clauson*, 314.
69. *Engel v. Vitale*, 370 U.S. 421, 435 (1962).
70. *Abington School District v. Schempp*, 295.
71. See text for note 47 *supra*.
72. *Walz v. Tax Commission*, 673.
73. *Marsh v. Chambers*, 463 U.S. 783, 786.
74. See Wade Clark Roof and William McKinney, *American Mainline Religion* (New Brunswick, N.J.: Rutgers University Press, 1987), 33–39.
75. Berger, *Sacred Canopy*, 107. See Mooney, *Public Virtue*, 1–2.
76. This definition is that of sociologist Jeffrey K. Hadden, "Religious Broadcasting and the Mobilization of the New Christian Right," *Journal for the Scientific Study of Religion* 26 (1987), 3.
77. See text for note 66 *supra*.
78. Jeffrey Stout, "Liberal Society," 55.
79. See text for note 37 of Part I *supra*.
80. Roof and McKinney, *American Mainline Religion*, 245.
81. Ibid., 247–251.

82. George M. Marsden, "Preachers of Paradox: The Religious New Right in Historical Perspective," in Mary Douglas and Steven M. Tipton, eds., *Religion and America* (Boston: Beacon Press, 1983), 150–168. This article is a summary of Marsden's much larger work, *Fundamentalism and American Culture* (New York: Oxford University Press, 1980).

83. *Mozert v. Hawkins County Public Schools*, 647 F. Supp. 1194 (1986); 827 F.2d 1058 (1987). On February 22, 1988, the Supreme Court denied Mozert's petition for a hearing of the case.

84. In *Torcaso v. Watkins*, 367 U.S. 488, 495, (1961), Justice Black held that theism was not required for a belief to be religious. He then said in a footnote that "among religions in the country which do not teach what would generally be considered a belief in the existence of God are Buddhism, Taoism, Ethical Culture, Secular Humanism and others."

85. *Smith v. Board of School Commissioners*, 665 F. Supp 939 (1987); 827 F.2d 684 (1987).

86. *Epperson v. Arkansas*, 393 U.S. 97 (1968), ruled that an Arkansas law proscribing the teaching of evolution in public schools was unconstitutional because its sole reason for doing so was that evolution was in conflict with "a particular religious doctrine."

87. See the historical overviews by Dorothy Nelkin, *The Creation Controversy* (Boston: Beacon Press, 1982), and Edward J. Larson, *Trial and Error: The American Controversy over Creation and Evolution* (New York: Oxford University Press, 1985).

88. See Marsden, "Preachers of Paradox," 164. The Morris quote is from Nelkin, *Creation Controversy*, 85.

89. As reported in the *Chronicle of Higher Education*, December 10, 1986.

90. *McLean v. Arkansas Board of Education*. The text of the Arkansas law, the District Court opinion, as well as a fascinating account of the courtroom battle, will all be found in Langdon Gilkey, *Creationism on Trial, Evolution and God at Little Rock* (New York: Harper & Row, 1985).

91. *Edwards v. Aguillard*, 482 U.S. 578, 591, 586-587, 629 (1987).

92. Miller, *The First Liberty*, 321.

93. De Tocqueville, *Democracy in America*, 291.

94. Gilbert K. Chesterton, *What I Saw in America* (New York: Dodd, Mead, 1922), 11–12.
95. *Holy Trinity Church v. United States*, 131 U.S. 457, 471 (1892).
96. *United States v. Macintosh*, 283 U.S. 605, 625 (1931).
97. *Zorach v. Clauson*, 313.
98. *Engel v. Vitale*, 370 U.S. 421, 425 (1962).
99. *Widmar v. Vincent*, 454 U.S. 263 (1981).
100. *Wallace v. Jaffree*, 472 U.S. 38, 59 (1985). Justice Stevens made this statement in the course of striking down an Alabama "minute of silence" statute because it manifested a "religious character" by stating its purpose to be "for meditation or silent prayer." Presumably if the mention of prayer had been omitted, the secular purpose of simply fostering meditation would have been recognized as legitimate.
101. *Abington School District v. Schempp*, 225.
102. *Edwards v. Aguillard*, 606-608.
103. The report, entitled "Religion in the Curriculum," is reprinted in its entirety in the *Journal of the American Academy of Religion* 55 (1987), 569–588.
104. See, for example, *Hunt v. McNair*, 413 U.S. 734 (1973).
105. *Zorach v. Clauson*, 313.
106. I am indebted here to the unpublished paper by Arlin M. Adams, retired judge of the Third Circuit Court of Appeals, "Accommodation and the Religious Clauses of the Constitution," and to Michael W. McConnell, "Accommodation of Religion," 1985 *Supreme Court Review*, 1–59.
107. The case was *Lemon v. Kurtzman*, 402 U.S. 602 (1971), but the test began its development as early as 1963 in the *Schempp* opinion. See note 51 *supra*.
108. *Walz v. Tax Commission*, 668–669.
109. Ibid., 673, 675. For an expanded treatment of this admirable opinion, see Mooney, *Public Virtue*, 42–45. It is ironic that Justice Douglas, who first broached the accommodation concept in *Zorach*, should have dissented from Burger's accommodation defense in *Walz*. But then, as William Lee Miller says of Douglas, his career through the religion cases resembled "the homeward journey of a New Year's Eve reveler." (*The First Liberty*, 303.)
110. The first statement is from *Walz*, 670, the second from *Lemon*, 612.

111. *Marsh* v. *Chambers*, 463 U.S. 783, 786, 792 (1983).
112. *Lynch* v.*Donnelly*, 465 U.S. 668, 673, 678, 679 (1984). This decision upheld the constitutionality of a Nativity scene display on public property in Pawtucket, Rhode Island.
113. *Widmar* v. *Vincent*, 263.
114. *Mueller* v. *Allen*, 463 U.S. 388, 399, 400 (1983).
115. *Aguilar* v. *Felton*, 473 U.S. 402, 413, 420, 431 (1985).
116. *Tilton* v. *Richardson*, 678.
117. Michael Walzer, *Interpretation and Social Criticism* (Cambridge, Mass.: Harvard University Press, 1986).
118. From an unpublished paper delivered in 1971, quoted by Andrew M. Greeley, "The Civil Religion of Ethnic Americans," *Religious Education* 70 (1975), 500–501.
119. *National Labor Relations Board* v. *Jones and Laughlin Steel Corp.*, 301 U.S. 1 (1937).
120. Brandeis was dissenting in *United States* v. *Moreland*, 258 U.S. 433, 441 (1922).
121. A recent attempt is that of Archibald Cox, *The Court and the Constitution* (Boston: Houghton Mifflin Company, 1987).
122. Alexander M. Bickel, *The Least Dangerous Branch* (Indianapolis: Bobbs-Merrill, 1962), 98–105.
123. C. Vann Woodward, *The Strange Career of Jim Crow*, 2nd ed. (New York: Oxford University Press, 1966), 20, 70.
124. See the insightful article by Ronald Dworkin, "The Bork Nomination," *New York Review*, August 13, 1987.
125. Irving R. Kaufman, of the Second Circuit Court of Appeals, "What Did the Founding Fathers Intend?" *New York Times Magazine*, February 23, 1986, 59; Justice Brennan's words are from an address at Georgetown University on October 12, 1985, reported in the *New York Times*, October 13, 1985.
126. Judge Charles E. Wyzanski of the U.S. District Court of Boston, "Judicial Review in America: Some Reflections," in Ronald K. L. Collins, ed., *Constitutional Government in America* (Durham, N.C.: Duke University Press, 1980), 485; quoted by Michael Kammen, *A Machine That Would Go of Itself* (New York: Vintage Books, 1987), xx.
127. Miller, *The First Liberty*, 316.
128. See her concurring opinion in *Wallace* v. *Jaffree*, 83.
129. Holmes, *Common Law*, 5. See the perceptive remarks on

this point by Charles M. Whelan, "The First Amendment: Its Present and Future," *Catholic Mind*, October 1976, 25-28.

130. Letter of November 21, 1808, in Saul K. Padover, ed., *The Complete Jefferson* (New York: Duell, Sloan and Pearce, 1943), 538.

131. Noonan, *The Believer*, xiii. In *Constitutional Faith* (Princeton: Princeton University Press, 1988) Sanford Levinson develops the interesting insight that the strains of interpretation we associate with Protestant and Catholic theology have their counterparts in constitutional law. The Protestant "temper of mind" has its analog for Levinson in constitutional commentary that treats the text as the basis of authority, in contrast to the Catholic "temper of mind" that finds this basis in the body of doctrine developed from the text and in the special weight given to Supreme Court decisions (as against those of other courts or other branches of government). These two strains can be separated, says Levinson, but advocates of each can almost always be found on the Supreme Court.

132. *Abington School District v. Schempp*, 226.

133. *Committee for Public Education and Religious Liberty v. Regan*, 444 U.S. 646, 662 (1980).

Part III: Education's Prism

1. Allan Bloom, *The Closing of the American Mind* (New York: Simon & Schuster, 1987), 382.

2. *To Secure the Blessings of Liberty*, a report of the National Commission on the Role and Future of State Colleges and Universities, reprinted in *Chronicle of Higher Education*, November 12, 1986; survey by the Education Commission of the States, reported by the *New York Times*, December 13, 1987; Chester R. Finn, Jr., and Diane Ravitch, *What Do Our 17-Year-Olds Know?* (New York: Harper & Row, 1987), reported in *Chronicle of Higher Education*, September 16, 1987.

3. Plato's words are from Book I of *Laws*, §643. Aristotle's principles of education will be found at the end of Book VII and the start of Book VIII of *Politics*. On classic education generally see Werner Jaeger, *Paideia: The Ideals of Greek Culture* (New York: Oxford University Press, 1945).

4. See Paul O. Kristeller, *Renaissance Thought and Its*

Sources (New York: Columbia University Press, 1979), 86–105, 169–181; Richard P. McKeon, "The Transformation of the Liberal Arts in the Renaissance," in Bernard Levi, ed., *Developments in the Early Renaissance* (Albany: State University of New York Press, 1972), 161–169.

5. I adapt here the insights of Bruce A. Kimball, *Orators and Philosophers* (New York: Teachers College Press, 1986).

6. Alfred North Whitehead, *The Aims of Education* (New York: New American Library, 1949), 58, 14.

7. George F. Kennan, *The Nuclear Delusion* (New York: Pantheon, 1982), 204.

8. Ibid., 205.

9. On these statistics see the sources used by Andrew Hacker in "The Decline of Higher Learning," *New York Review*, February 13, 1986.

10. William J. Bennett, *To Reclaim a Legacy* (Washington, D.C.: National Endowment for the Humanities, 1984); Frederick Rudolph et al., *Integrity in the College Curriculum* (Washington, D.C.: Association of American Colleges, 1985); *Involvement in Learning: Realizing the Potential of American Higher Education* (Washington, D.C.: National Institute of Education, 1985).

11. Ernest L. Boyer, *College: The Undergraduate Experience in America* (New York: Harper & Row, 1987), 2. This is also the main argument of Lynne V. Cheney, chair of the National Endowment for the Humanities, in her "Humanities in America: A Report to the President, the Congress, and the American People," reprinted in *Chronicle of Higher Education*, September 21, 1988. Her views have been vigorously disputed by a 1989 report of the American Council of Learned Societies, "Speaking for the Humanities," reprinted in *Chronicle of Higher Education*, January 11, 1989.

12. E. D. Hirsch, Jr., *Cultural Literacy: What Every American Needs to Know* (Boston: Houghton Mifflin, 1987), 21.

13. Martha Nussbaum, "Undemocratic Vistas," *New York Review*, November 5, 1987.

14. Bloom, *Closing*, 38–39.

15. Ibid., 33.

16. See *Tilton v. Richardson*, 403 U.S. 672 (1971).

17. *West Virginia Board of Education* v. *Barnette*, 319 U.S. 624, 642 (1943).

18. Justice Holmes was dissenting in *Abrams* v. *United States*, 250 U.S. 616, 630 (1919). Bloom ridicules this statement because, he says, it renounced seeking for a principle to determine which speech or conduct is legally tolerable in a democracy and opted for the preservation of public order as the only common good. (*Closing*, 28). Bloom here ignores the obvious distinction between public morality, which is enforced by many agencies in society and whose objective is indeed the common good, and one particular enforcing agency, namely law, whose moral scope has always been limited to the realm of public order.

19. *United States* v. *Associated Press*, 52 F. Supp. 362, 372 (1943).

20. "A Bill for Establishing Religious Freedom," in Merrill D. Peterson, ed., *The Portable Thomas Jefferson*, 253.

21. Alexander Meiklejohn, *Free Speech and Its Relation to Self-Government* (New York: Harper & Brothers, 1948), 32.

22. See the comments of Alexander M. Bickel, *The Morality of Consent* (New Haven, Conn.: Yale University Press, 1975), 70–72.

23. Werner Heisenberg, *Physics and Philosophy* (New York: Harper & Brothers, 1958), 53. Quoted by Peggy Rosenthal, *Words and Values* (New York: Oxford University Press, 1984), 124. Rosenthal's study of the word *relativity* is fascinating, but marred by her basic hostility to the concept and her preoccupation with defending the existence of truths that are absolute.

24. David Tracy, *Plurality and Ambiguity* (New York: Harper & Row, 1987), 50. See Rosenthal, *Words and Values*, 150–153.

25. Ninian Smart, "Relativism in Ethics," in James F. Childress and John Macquarrie, eds., *The Westminster Dictionary of Christian Ethics* (Philadelphia: Westminster Press, 1986), 532.

26. John Kenneth Galbraith, *The Age of Uncertainty* (Boston: Houghton Mifflin, 1977), 7.

27. Richard Joseph Barnet, "Reporter at Large," *New Yorker*, March 17, March 31, April 7, 1980.

28. Boyer, *College*, 6.

29. Michael Buckley, "The University and the Concern for

Justice: The Search for a New Humanism," *Thought* 57 (1982), 219–233.

30. Ernest L. Boyer and Fred M. Hechinger, *Higher Learning in the Nation's Service* (Washington, D.C.: Carnegie Foundation, 1981), 43, 47–48.

31. See Paul Harrison, *The Third World Tomorrow* (New York: Pilgrim Press, 1983); Robert L. McCan, *World Economy and World Hunger* (Washington, D.C.: University Publications of America, 1982); William J. Bryon, ed., *The Causes of World Hunger* (New York: Paulist Press, 1982).

32. Gertrude Himmelfarb, *The Idea of Poverty* (New York: Knopf, 1984), 332.

33. The "poverty line" is a standard elaborated in 1964 by the Census Bureau and the Social Security Administration to determine whether a family can be officially called "poor." It is based upon the cost of an economy food plan prepared by the Agriculture Department in the early 1960s. This plan was a balanced diet of nutritious foods available at minimum cost — rice, beans, bread, processed cheese, etc. Because the department had concluded that poor families spent about a third of their income on food, the Census Bureau took this diet as a norm, estimated its cost and multiplied by three. The result was the poverty line. Updating this figure each year by the Consumer Price Index, the bureau said that in 1987 an annual income of $11,611 constituted this edge of poverty for a family of four. It has been noted often that this current measure most likely understates rather than overstates the number of poor. A consumer expenditure survey from the early 1970s indicates that only about one-fifth of poor people's outlays goes for food. Hence if the cost of the economy plan were multiplied by five instead of three, the poverty line would be much higher.

34. See *New York Times*, November 19, 1987.

35. See the radically contradictory interpretation of identical data by two serious sociologists: William Julius Wilson, *The Truly Disadvantaged: The Inner City, the Underclass, and Public Policy* (Chicago: University of Chicago Press, 1987); Charles Murray, *Losing Ground: American Social Policy, 1950–1980* (New York: Basic Books, 1984).

36. On unemployable persons and the feminization of poverty, see Ken Auletta, *The Underclass* (New York: Random House,

1982); Michael Harrington, *The New American Poverty* (New York: Holt, Rinehart & Winston, 1984). On the terror of homelessness see Jonathan Kozol, *Rachel and Her Children: Homeless Families in America* (New York: Crown Publishers, 1988).

37. Whitehead, *Aims of Education*, 27–52.

38. See, for example, the extensive study by three social scientists at the University of Michigan's Institute for Social Research, Joseph Veroff, Elizabeth Douvan, and Richard A. Kulka, *The Inner American* (New York: Basic Books, 1981), especially pp. 529ff.

39. The full text will be found in *Chronicle of Higher Education*, January 6, 1988.

40. Geneen is quoted by two professors of business, William G. Scott and Terrence R. Mitchell, "The Moral Failure of Management Education," *Chronicle of Higher Education*, December 11, 1985. See also the perceptive article by James Gaffney, "Moral Views and Moral Viewpoints," *America*, January 23, 1988.

41. *The American Freshman: National Norms for Fall 1987* (Los Angeles: Higher Education Research Institute, 1987), cited in *Chronicle of Higher Education*, January 20, 1988.

42. Daniel Yankelovich, *New Rules*, 227, 249.

43. See text for note 37 of Part I *supra*.

44. Ross J. S. Hoffman and Paul Levack, eds., *Burke's Politics* (New York: Knopf, 1970), 71.

45. See the perceptive comments by Carol J. Greenhouse, "Teaching America: Community, Pluralism and Law," *Focus* 3 (1987), 1–9.

46. See Edward B. Fiske, "How Education Came to Be a Campaign Issue," *New York Times*, January 3, 1988.

47. See text for note 56 of Part II *supra*.

48. A good example of a religious critique of the U.S. economy from the viewpoint of its effect on the poor is the pastoral letter of the American Catholic Bishops, *Economic Justice for All* (Washington, D.C.: National Conference of Catholic Bishops, 3rd draft, 1986). For further analysis of the economic issue see Bradley R. Schiller, *The Economics of Poverty and Discrimination* (Englewood Cliffs, N.J.: Prentice-Hall, 1984).

INDEX

Abingdon School District v. *Schempp*, 66, 79, 80, 83, 95, 167 n.51
Abolitionist movement, 23, 54–55
Abortion issue, 18, 22–23, 30
Academic freedom, 91
Accommodation, 67, 80–81, 98–104, 114, 132
"Act for Establishing Religious Freedom" (Jefferson), 42–43
Adams, John, 53
Adamson v. *California*, 166–67 n.44
Agriculture, U.S. Department of: determination of poverty line, 175 n.33
Ahlstrom, Sydney, 5, 57–58
Aims of Education, The (Whitehead), 122, 144
Alienation between educated taste and human sensibility, 138–39
Ambiguity of knowledge, toleration of, 128–37
Ames, Fisher, 46, 47
Anthropology, cultural relativism of, 135
Anti-Federalists, 45
Antilegalism, 25
Arendt, Hannah, 5
Areté, 120
Aristotle, 120
Arkansas, 89, 90, 169 nn.86, 90
Art, insight provided by, 144
Articles of faith, 1st Amendment provisions as, 49, 164 n.17
Articles of peace, 1st Amendment provisions as, 49, 164 n.17

Assimilation of immigrants, 153
Association for Supervision and Curriculum Development, 96–97
Auerbach, Jerold, 7
Austin, John, 6

Backus, Isaac, 42
Bailyn, Bernard, 41–42
Baptists, 42
Barnet, Richard, 136
Belief, freedom of, 67
Beliefs, 128, 133, 135–36
Bell, Terrel, 118
Bellah, Robert, 17, 84, 148–49
Benevolent neutrality: as approach to religious pluralism, 80
Bennett, William J., 118
Berger, Peter, 19–20
Berman, Harold, 4, 25
Berns, Walter, 48
Bible: fundamentalist belief in inerrancy of, 86; reading in public schools, 69, 73, 74, 79, 94; study of in public schools, 95–96
Biblical religion/tradition, 17, 26, 148–49
Bickel, Alexander, 108
"Bill for Appointing Days of Public Fasting and Thanksgiving" (Jefferson), 43
Bill of Rights, 45–49, 109; applicability of procedural rights to the states, 60–61, 166 n.43; substantive rights incorporated into 14th Amendment, 61–63, 109, 166

177

nn.43, 44. *See also* First
    Amendment
Black, Hugo, 80, 95, 159 n.22,
    166–67 n.44, 169 n.84; interpretation of establishment
    clause, 64–66, 67, 77–78
Blacks: intent of framers of 14th
    Amendment toward, 110. *See
    also* Racial discrimination
    and segregation
Bloom, Allan, 131, 133, 174
    n.18; criticisms of higher
    education, 117–18, 126–27,
    128–29, 136–37
Blue laws, 52
Boorstin, Daniel, 53
Boyer, Ernest L., 117–18, 126,
    127, 138
Brennan, William J., Jr., ix–x,
    91, 103, 111; on application
    of 1st and 14th Amendments,
    68, 80, 167 n.51; response to
    Meese's attack, 37–38,
    161–62 n.1
Brewer, David, 93–94
Brown, Robert McAfee, 86
Brown v. *Board of Education*,
    75, 108, 109–10
Buckley, Michael, 139
Burger, Warren E., ix, 71; on
    accommodation, 80, 98,
    100–102, 104
Burke, Edmund, 149–50
Business: loss of respect for
    values and ethical behavior
    in, 146–47, 153
Busing to parochial schools,
    64–65, 66

Cantwell v. *Connecticut*, 62,
    65, 67
Capitalism, 55, 56, 153–54
Career: preparation for, 121–22,
    123, 125–26, 127; success in
    as concern of students, 147
Carnegie Foundation Report on
    Americans as ill-informed,
    140

Catholics, 16, 72, 74, 172 n.131
Census Bureau: figures on
    poverty, 142–43, 175 n.33
Chaplaincy system, 44, 48, 66,
    101
Cheney, Lynne V., 173 n.11
Child labor laws, 112
Chosen people, Americans as,
    53–54
Christian nation, U.S. viewed
    as, 50–52, 93
Church: European and
    American use of term, 40
Church and state, 39–40. *See
    also* Religion, relationship of
    to government
Churches. *See* Religious institutions
Citizenship, 55–59; in global
    village, 139–42; higher
    education as initiation into,
    117, 119–28; higher education as preparation for,
    137–48, 155
Civic virtue, 42, 43
Civil communities: relationship
    with religious communities,
    162 n.2
Civil life: involvement in, 149;
    19th-century Protestantism as
    permeating, 51–59
Civil rights, 10–11, 21, 23,
    108–10, 145–46
Civil War, 54–55, 129
Clark, Tom, 69, 95–96, 115
Classicists, 133, 136
*Closing of the American Mind,
    The* (Bloom), 117–18,
    126–27, 128–29, 174 n.18
Coercion: in establishment
    clause violations, 65, 75, 79,
    88, 99
Coherence in curriculum,
    127–28
College (Boyer), 117–18, 126,
    127, 138
Colleges: religion courses at
    public supported, 97–98. *See
    also* Higher education

Index

Colonists, 40–42, 53, 149–50
Commentaries on the Constitution (Story), 51
Commerce, concern for: relationship to public virtue, 56–57, 58
Commerce clause, 107
Commission on National Challenge to Education, 146
Common good, 6, 39, 85, 124, 133, 149; concern for, 56–57, 119, 151; interconnection between law, religion, and higher education in search for, 119, 148–55; interconnection between religion and law in search for, 3, 19–28, 35; preservation of public order as the, 174 n.18; relationship to pluralism, x–xi, 94; religion as sensitive to, 152–54
Common law, English, 6
Community, 145–48, 149–50
Community colleges, 125, 127
Compromise, 48, 132, 162 n.4; in interrelationship between government and religion, 94–104
Congress, U.S., 106–7, 111; disputed intent in 14th Amendment, 63, 166–67 n.44; First, 45–49, 163 n.17
Conscience, 4, 21, 77; freedom of, 43, 49, 67, 73–74; proposal for amendment concerning, 46, 47
Consensus, x–xi, 30–31, 33, 36; words of 1st Amendment as representing, 47, 49
Conservatives, x, 110–11, 143, 144
Conservativism, religious (Postliberalism), 15–16
Constitution, U.S., ix–x, xi–xii, 1, 5–6, 76; changing interpretations of, 37–38, 106–16; safeguards in, 35, 57. *See also* Bill of Rights; *amendments by number*

Constitutional Faith (Levinson), 172 n.131
Constitutional law, 106–16, 173 n.131; and changing interpretation of establishment clause, 38–39, 59–71
Constitutions, colonial, 41
Constructionists, strict, 111
Contract rights, 4, 112
Conventions, moral principles embodied in, 135–36
Conversion experience, 86
Courts, 64, 69–70; federal, 64, 87–89, 112. *See also* Supreme Court, U.S.
"Creation science" controversy, 29, 89–91
Critical analysis of the human situation, 141–43
Critical legal theory, 7–8
Cultural Literacy (Hirsch), 117–18, 126, 127
Cultural relativism, 128, 135
Culture, ix–x, 1–3, 16–17, 21–27, 149; effect on religion, 11–19; higher education's connection to, 120, 126–27, 155; 19th-century Protestant hegemony in, 50–59, 71; secularization of, 3–6; use of term, 1–2
Curran, Charles, 16
Curricula, 117–18, 122–23, 146–47, 155; criticisms of, 126–27; need to serve diverse population, 124–28
Curry, Thomas, 50–51
Curtis, Michael Kent, 166–67 n.44
Customs, moral principles embodied in, 135–36

Death penalty statutes, 9–10
Declaration of Independence, 43, 56–57
De facto establishment, 50
Democratic tradition, relativism in, 129–33

Index

Denominations, 2, 70
De Toqueville, Alexis, 28, 58–59
Diggins, John, 165–66 n.30
Disestablishment, 11–19, 34, 40–59; compromise in conflicts concerning, 93–104; as legal synonym for secularization, 12–13, 18; moral pluralism as, 82–92; nationalization of, 59–71, 105; role of Protestant hegemony's breakdown in, 71–82. *See also* Establishment; Establishment clause
Dissenters (Sectarians), 42, 45
Divine destiny, sense of, 53–54
Douglas, William O., 1, 80, 93–94, 99, 170 n.109
Dred Scott decision, 108
Due process clause of 5th Amendment, 60–61
Due process clause of 14th Amendment, 60–63, 67–71, 106

Ecclesiastical language, 16
Economics, 3, 13, 21, 23, 145; moral dimensions, 146–47; and 19th-century Protestant hegemony, 55, 56; rights, 21, 61, 166 n.37
Education, xi, 29, 73, 117–19, 126, 151–52; legal, 6–7. *See also* Higher education; Public schools
Education for Economic Security Act (1984), 15, 159 n.23
Egalitariansim, 6, 21, 75–79, 125–26, 129, 150
Einstein, Albert, 134
Elitism as threat to higher education, 119, 137–44, 148, 151, 152
Employees, treatment of, 61, 166 n.37
Employers, rights of, 61, 112, 166 n.37

Enlightenment, the, 45, 48, 56, 150, 162 n.4
"Enthusiasm," religious, 52
Epistemology, effects of concepts of relativity on, 134–35
Epperson v. *Arkansas*, 169 n.86
Equality, 6, 21, 75–79, 125–26, 129, 150
Equal protection clause of 14th Amendment, 70, 106, 110
Equal-time strategy: in "creation science" fight, 89, 90–91
Establishment, 29, 60, 77–79; in colonies, 42; in states, 45, 49, 51, 59. *See also* Disestablishment; Establishment clause
Establishment clause, 37–116; early application to federal government only, 59; interpretation of, 104–8, 112–16; interpretation of in 1940s, 62–66; and issues of religion in public schools, 95, 96; nationalization of, 62–71, 105, 167 n.51; text, 46; use to protect unbelief, 78–79; use to rule in "creation science" teaching controversy, 90–91; "zone" of accommodation between free exercise clause and, 98–104. *See also* Disestablishment; Establishment; First Amendment
Ethicists on moral judgments, 135
Ethics: college course in, 147. *See also* Morality
Ethos, 50, 72, 135–36
Evangelicals, 52–53, 78, 86. *See also* Fundamentalists
Everson v. *Board of Education*, 64–67, 74, 77, 81, 114
Evolutionary theory, 134; teaching of, 89, 90–91, 169 nn.86, 90
Exodus, story of the: colonists seen as reliving, 53–54

Index 181

Expression, freedom of, 21, 130–32

Fairman, Charles, 166–67 n.44
Federal government, ix, 59, 73–74, 75–76, 107. *See also* Government
Federalist Papers, 44, 45, 57, 104
Federalists, 45, 163 n.12
Federal territories, 60
Femininization of poverty, 143
Fifth Amendment, 60–61, 166 n.43
Financial success, 26–27, 84, 147
First Amendment, 41–49, 75, 114–15, 164 n.17; enactment, 45–49; guaranteed liberties embraced by 14th Amendment, 62–63; as protection of unbelief, 78–79; rights of protected from state impairment, 62–63, 67; religion clauses, 11, 51, 96 (*See also* Establishment clause; Free exercise clause); and secular humanism case, 88–89; secular humanism as religion for purposes of, 88–89, 169 n. 84; text, 46. *See also* Speech, freedom of
Food distribution in underdeveloped countries, 141–42
Food plan used in determination of poverty line, 175 n.33
Foreign investment in third world, 141–42
Founders/framers, 56–57, 165–66 n.30; interpretations of intent in 14th Amendment, 37, 81, 105, 109–11
Founders'/framers' intent in 1st Amendment, 40–49, 81, 93; changing interpretations of, 37, 65, 71, 78, 105, 113–14

Fourteenth Amendment, 40, 63, 105, 106, 114, 166–67 n.44; changing interpretations of, 37–38, 109–10, 111; due process clause, 60–63, 67–71, 106; as protection for unbelief, 78; as providing legal dignity for blacks, 55; substantive rights incorporated into, 61–63; use to apply 1st Amendment to the states, 62–71, 74–75, 167 n.51; use to extend federal limitations on state action, 73, 74–75
Frankfurter, Felix, 68, 80, 166–67 n.44
Franklin, Benjamin, 53
Free exercise clause, 38, 39, 47, 68, 73–75; application in *Everson* case, 64–65; ellipses in interpretation of, 105–6, 112–15; incorporated into 14th Amendment, 62–71; text, 46; "zone" of accommodation between establishment clause and, 98–104. *See also* First Amendment
Friedman, Lawrence, 9, 10–11
Functional illiteracy, 118
Fundamentalists, 14–15, 16, 18, 29–30, 34; challenge to moral pluralism, 85–91

Galbraith, John Kenneth, 136
Geneen, Harold S., 147
Generality of intent, 110–11
Gitlow v. *New York*, 62
Global village, citizenship in, 139–42
Good human life, teaching of, 128, 131–32
Government, 4, 41, 73–74, 85, 94, 120; distinction between society and, 39; loss of respect for values and ethical behavior in, 146–47; 19th-

century attitudes toward as religious, 50–57; role in society, 150–52. *See also* Federal government; States
Government, relationship of to religion, 19, 21, 39–40, 64, 81, 83; accommodation and compromise necessary in, 93–104; as constantly changing, 105–6, 107–8, 112–16; effects of fundamentalist challenge to moral pluralism, 85–91; under First Amendment, 11–12
Grain exports to third world, 142
Grand jury indictment requirement of 5th Amendment, 166 n.43
Greek tradition, 14; of liberal education, 120, 121–22
Greenawalt, Kent, 31–32

Hand, Learned, 130
Handy, Robert, 50, 52–53, 56, 71
Harrington, Mona, 35
Hatch, Orrin, 15
Hegemony, Protestant, 50–59, 71–82
Heisenberg, Werner, 134
Herberg, Will, 72, 153
Higher education, 117–19; elitism and value neutrality as threats to, 119, 137–48; as initiation into citizenship, 120–28; as intersecting with law and religion in search for common good, 148–55; and tolerating the ambiguity of knowledge, 128–29, 131–33, 135–37
Himmelfarb, Gertrude, 142
Hirsch, E. D., Jr., 117–18, 126, 127
History, 3–4, 24, 118, 134–35
Holmes, Oliver Wendell, Jr., 6, 115, 130, 174 n.18

Holt, Rhinehart, and Winston basic reading series controversy, 88
Homelessness, 23, 140
Homosexuals, 18; rights of, 23, 30, 110, 111
Howe, Marke de Wolfe, 76, 78–79
Human, the: absolutized in the secular, 83
Human condition, 139–43; need for critical analysis of, 141–48; need for sensitivity to, 138–39, 155
Humanism, 13–15, 83, 120–21, 127
Humanities: role in liberal education, 121, 122–23
Human rights, 21, 92
Hunger, global, 141–42

Idea of Poverty, The, (Himmelfarb), 142
Identity, religious, 15, 85
Illiteracy, 118
Immigrants, 72, 153
Income tax, state: deductions for educational expenses, 102
"Indirect aid" to religion, 66
Individualism, 17–18, 27, 34, 55, 149–50; as primary moral language, 84–85; relationship to public life, 25–27, 29; shift from community values to, 145–48
Individuality, law as protector of, 150–51
Instrumentality of law, 7–8
Intellectual growth, 144; role in liberal education, 121–23, 124–25
Isolation of higher education students and institutions, 138–44

Jackson, Robert, 106, 129–30
Jefferson, Thomas, 53, 56, 114,

130, 150; meaning of disestablishment for, 65, 66; on religion clauses, 115; views on religion, 41 42–43
Jehovah's Witnesses, 65
Jews, 14, 72, 74, 113
Jim Crow laws, 110
Judaeo-Christian tradition, 72, 82–84, 85, 87, 96
Judicial review, limit to power of, 111–12
Jury trial guarantee of 7th Amendment, 166 n.43
Justice, 21, 29, 36, 111, 124, 151; commitment to 145–46, 154; denial of as issue for religion, 22–23; need for sensitivity to, 140–43

Kennan, George, 123, 124
King, Martin Luther, Jr., 23
Knowledge, toleration of ambiguity of, 128–37
Küng, Hans, 16

Laissez-faire, 56, 61, 112
Law, 3–11, 21, 25, 34, 184 n.18; defined by Holmes, 6; interaction with religion, 1–3, 19–36; interconnection with religion and higher education in search for the common good, 119, 149–52; 19th-century use to impose Protestant morality, 52, 60; relationship to social change, 8–11, 155; roles in society, 150–52; sense of social responsibility, 24–26, 27; tradition of natural rights and equality under, 129; use of term, 2. See also Constitutional law
Laws (Plato), 120
League of Women Voters, 151–52
Legal analysis: as problem in establishment cases, 67–71

Legal discourse: moral discourse as part of, 21–22
Legal disestablishment, "first disestablishment" as, 72–73
Legal education, 6–7
Legalism, 25
Legal mind, 7, 20–21
Legal positivism, 5–7, 8
Legal realism, 6–8, 24
Legislative branch; inability to break political stalemates, 108. See also Congress, U.S.
Leland, John, 42
Lemon test, 99–100, 102–4
Levinson, Sanford, 172 n.131
Levy, Leonard W., 163 n.12
Liberal education, 124–28; criticisms of contemporary, 128–29, 133; study of religion in, 152–53; traditions in, 120–24. See also Higher education
Liberalism, classic, 57
Liberalism, political, 32
Liberals, x, 110–11, 143
Liberty, ix, 41–42, 57, 61; deprivation of by infringement of establishment clause, 67–70, 167 n.51
Lincoln, Abraham, 54–55
"Line of separation" (Madisonian metaphor), 66
Literature, insight provided by, 144
Livermore, Samuel, 46, 47
Llewellyn, Karl, 25
Local communities, 59–60; applications of establishment clause to, 63–71, 74–75; government intervention in, 85, 105
Lochner v. New York, 166 n.37
Locke, John 56
Louisiana, 89, 90–91
Lovin, Robin, 30, 31
Lutheranism, 20

McCollum case, 79–80

184   Index

McGuffey's *Readers*, 57–58
MacIntyre, Alasdair, 30
MacIver, Robert, 8
Macro-morality, need for, 16–17, 34
Madison, James, 41, 56, 57, 107, 114; meaning of disestablishment for, 65, 66; role in framing 1st Amendment, 41, 45–48, 49; views on religion, 41, 42–44
Manifest destiny, 55
Market: control of under commerce clause, 107
Marsden, George, 86, 90
Marty, Martin, 13, 16, 92
Massachusetts, 51
Maximum hour laws, 112
May, Henry F., 162 n.4
Meanings, shared, 29–32
Meese, Edwin, 37–38
Meiklejohn, Alexander, 131
Membership, concept of, 150
Memorandum to the 41st President, 146
"Memorial and Remonstrance Against Religious Assessments" (Madison), 43
Methodists, 42
Micro-morality, need for, 16
Miller, William Lee, 72, 92, 112, 163 n.11, 170 n.109; on Madison's support for religious pluralism, 44–45; on Protestantism in 19th-century American culture, 51–52
Minimum wage laws, 112
Minnesota, 102–3
"Minute of silence" statutes, 95, 170 n.100
Missouri, University of at Kansas City, 102
Mobile, Ala., 88–89
Modernism, 86
Modernity, 14–15, 16–17, 34, 133
Moral discourse: as part of legal discourse, 21–22
Morality, 18, 28, 113, 132–33, 144, 155; breakdown of common agreement on, 82–92; education in, 57; macro- and micro-morality, 16–17; Protestant, 50, 52–53, 55–59; relationship to law, 5, 9, 24–27; principles needed for examination of human experience, 144–48; and responsibility for the common good, 22, 174 n.18; values, 21, 110–11, 135–36. *See also* Pluralism, moral
Moral language, 84–85
Mores, liberation of, 144–45
Mormons, 60, 74
Morris, Henry, 90
Moslems, 113
Murray, John Courtenay, 49, 164 n.17

"Nation at Risk, A," 118
Nativity scene display, 171 n.112
Natural rights, 128–29
Natural sciences, 121, 122–23, 128, 133, 144
Nature, secularized view of, 3–4
Neutrality as approach to religious pluralism, 77–81
New Jersey, 64–65
New York, 166 n.37
Niebuhr, H. Richard, 1–2, 20
Niebuhr, Reinhold, 35–36
Northwest Ordinance of 1787: 1789 readoption, 48

O'Connor, Sandra Day, 104, 113
Openness, Bloom's criticism of, 128–29, 131, 133
Ordinary life, isolation from, 138–44
Original sin, 35
Others, diverse social groups seen as, 150–51

Overpopulation in third world, 141

Parochialism, 126, 138
Parochial schools, 64–65, 66, 81, 103–4
Peaceable assembly, right of, 62
Penn, William, 42
Pennsylvania, 42, 66
Personality, human: development in liberal education, 121–22
Physics, relativity concept in, 133–34
Plato, 120
Plessy v. *Ferguson*, 108
Pluralism, x–xi, 5–6, 119, 129–33, 137, 150
Pluralism, moral, 22, 24, 34, 94, 115, 135–36; fundamentalism's challenge to, 85–91; as the "third disestablishment," 82–92
Pluralism, religious, 11–12, 70, 91–92, 94, 96, 129; as catalyst for moral pluralism, 82–83; effects on interaction of law and religion, 20; as part of American ethos, 135–36; religious liberty as corollary of, 38; role of growth in "second disestablishment," 72–82; roots, 19, 115; as security for religious rights, 44–45, 163 n.10
Political science, 147
Politics, 13, 27, 35, 51, 86, 118; moral dimensions of, 146–47; preferences of individual justices, 110–11; religious dimension, 53–57
Politics (Aristotle), 120
Polygamy statutes, 60
Poor, the, 23, 140–43, 151, 175 n.33
Positivism, legal, 5–7, 8, 21, 24
Post-liberalism (Religious conservatism), 15–16

Poverty, 75, 140–43; in the U.S., 140, 142–143, 153, 175 n.33
Poverty line, 142–43, 175 n.33
Powell, Lewis, 96, 102
Powell, Thomas Reed, 7
Power, 7–8, 10–11, 35, 83, 151; ecclesiastical, 41–42; political, 5, 8, 41, 44
Prayer before legislative sessions, 80
Prayer in public schools, 29, 70, 73, 74, 80–81; compromise solutions to issue of, 94–95, 170 n.100; *Schempp* case, 79
Presbyterians, 42
Press, freedom of, 62, 78
Privacy, right of, 111
Privatization: of faith, 85; of religion, 13, 18; of religious experience, 19
Procedural rights, 61, 68, 166 n.43
Property rights, 4, 67–68, 112
Prophetic tradition, 22–23, 153
Protestant-Catholic-Jew (Herberg), 72, 153
Protestantism, 4, 16, 20, 74, 172 n.131; hegemony in 19th century, 50–59, 71–82; limited scope of the sacred, 19–20. *See also* Fundamentalists
Psychology, effects on of concepts of relativity, 134–35
Public days of prayer and fasting, 43–44
Public discourse, x–xi, 26–33
Public issues, 85, 140
Public order, 20–21, 150, 174 n.18
Public property, Nativity scene display on, 171 n.112
Public schools, 60, 73–74, 79–80, 94–98; Bible reading in, 69, 73, 74, 79, 94; Fundamentalist legal actions relating to, 87–91; Protestantism's support for,

186 Index

52–53, 57–58; use of teachers in parochial schools, 103–4. *See also* Prayer in public schools
Public sphere, 19–21, 26–27, 28–33, 36
Public virtue, 17, 56–57, 165–66 n.30

Quakers, 42

Racial discrimination and segregation, 55, 75, 76, 108–10, 113; fight against, 23, 145–46
Rehnquist, William, 70, 91, 102–3
Relativism, 133–37, 174 n.23; attacks on, 128–29, 133; cultural, 128, 135
Released-time programs for religious instructions, 79–80, 99
Relevance, demands for, 138–39
Religion, 28–30, 48, 51, 83, 115, 155; and commitment to values, 152–53; culture's effect on, 11–19; effects of secularization on, 82–85; Federalist view on, 45, 163 n. 12; as integral dimension to political experience, 51, 53–57; interaction with law, 1–3, 19–36; interconnection with law and higher education in search for the common good, 119, 149–50, 152–54; message of, 154; as permeating civil life, 51–59; as regarded prior to 1787, 40–45; released time for instruction in, 79–80, 99; secular humanism as form of, 88–89, 169 n. 84; as source of identity, 153; study of in higher education, 97–98, 121, 152–53; as subject matter of secular education, 95–98; teaching about differentiated from teaching of, 95–98; use of term, 2
Religion, relationship of to government, ix, 39–40, 66, 81, 83; accommodation and compromise necessary in, 93–104; as affected by fundamentalist challenge to moral pluralism, 85–91; as constantly changing, 105–6, 107–8, 112–16; end of regional diversity in, 64; in 19th century, 50–57
Religion clauses of 1st Amendment, 11, 51, 96. *See also* Establishment clause; Free exercise clause
Religio-secular mentality, 13, 18, 28
Religious communities: relationship with civil communities, 162 n.2
Religious freedom/liberty, 12, 19, 50, 73, 76, 95; establishment prohibition as assurance of, 65–66, 74–75; Founders' agreement on need for, 43, 49; and individualism, 149–50; and legal analysis of establishment cases, 67–71. *See also* Free exercise clause
Religious holidays, public observance of, 66
Religious indifferentism, 164 n.17
Religious institutions, 22–24, 57–59, 73–74, 84–85; character of, 11–19; concern with public life, 27–36; secularization as escape from domination of, 3–4, 6, 82–85; tax exemption for, 80, 101
Religiousness, 2, 13–14
Renaissance tradition of liberal education, 120–22
Republicanism, classical, 17, 26,

56–57, 148–49, 150, 165–66 n.30
Restlessness, social and psychological, 145, 148
Revivalists, 52, 86
Rhode Island, 42
Ricoeur, Paul, 106
Rights, 6, 21–22, 26–27, 41, 92. *See also* Civil rights; Contract rights; Economics: rights
Rituals, 54, 135–36
Rives, William C., 163 n. 10
Roe v. *Wade*, 22
Roof, Wade Clark, 17–18
Rosenthal, Peggy, 174 n.23

Sabbatarians, 74
Sabbath observance, 52, 73
Sacred, the, 19–20, 24, 83
Scalia, Antonin, 91
Schempp case *(Abingdon School District* v. *Schempp)*, 66, 79, 80, 83, 95, 167 n. 51
Science, 3–4, 13, 128–29, 133, 134
Sciences courses: evolution vs. "creation science" in, 89–91
Second Amendment, 166 n.43
Second Great Awakening, 52
Sectarianism, ix, 15–16, 29–30, 150
Sectarians (Dissenters), 42, 45
Secular humanism, 13–15, 86–89, 159 n.22, 169 n.84
Secularism, ix, 14, 34, 72, 78–80, 83, 87
Secularists, 13–15, 86, 113
Secularity, 83–85
Secularization, 14–15, 20, 27, 34, 82–85; disestablishment as legal synonym for, 12–13, 18; effects on law, 3–11; and fundamentalism, 85–91
Segregation, racial. *See* Racial discrimination and segregation
Self-fulfillment, 26, 84–85, 121, 123–24, 149; ethos of, 145, 148
Self-government, 56, 131
Self-interest, 17, 56, 58, 151
Separate but equal treatment for blacks, legalization of, 108
Seventh Amendment, 166 n.43
Shaw, George Bernard, 1
Single issue politics, 29–30
Skepticism, 121, 133, 135–36
Slavery, 41, 109–10, 113
Social change, 8–11, 34
Social ethic, 2, 148
Social institutions, 8, 85, 144–45, 152, 153–54
Social justice. *See* Justice
Social legislation, initial invalidation of, 112
Social sciences, 121, 122–23, 128, 133, 144
Social values, 7, 85
Society, 12, 25–27, 33, 39, 132, 152–53; attacks on, 129; changing role of government and religion in, 105, 108; concern for problems of, 17, 140–43, 154–55; diversity of reflected in higher education, 127–28; relationship to law, 8–11, 25–26; Renaissance tradition aimed at reform of, 120–21; secularization of, 3–6, 82–83; "soft structure" of, 58
Sociological disestablishment, "second disestablishment" as, 71–82
Sophie's Choice (film), 137–38
Speech, freedom of, 21, 62, 65, 78, 130–32
Sponsorship of religion: distinguished from accommodation, 99–104
State, European and American use of term, 39–40
State college systems, 125, 127
States, 49, 51–53, 57, 60, 70, 166 n. 43; alternative inter-

pretations of establishment restrictions on, 69–71; applicability of 1st Amendment to, 38–39, 59, 63–71, 114; effects of 14th Amendment on, 60–71, 74–75, 109; establishments in, 45, 49, 51, 59; laws concerning teaching "creation science," 89, 90–91
Stevens, John Paul, 38, 95, 161–62 n.1, 170 n.100
Stewart, Potter, 79, 83
Story, Joseph, 51
Stout, Jeffrey, 27, 84
Sturm, Donald, 25
Subjectivism, 85, 134–35
Substantive rights, 61–62, 63, 68, 166–67 n.44
Sunday closing laws, 73–74
Supreme Court, U.S., 74–81, 87, 92, 105, 107, 159 n.22; changing constitutional interpretation, 106–16; and "creation science" controversy, 89, 90–91, 96; decisions on establishment cases, 41, 64–71, 79, 129, 164 n.51; Meese's attack on, 37; need for willingness to compromise, 94–96, 97, 98–104; on secular humanism as form of religion, 88–89, 169 n.84; use of accommodation, 98–104, 114; use of 14th Amendment to extend federal limitations on state action, 61–71, 73, 74–75, 166–67 n.44; value judgments in *Roe v. Wade*, 22
Sutherland, George, 93–94

Taxation: allowances for school fees, 66; exemption for churches, 66, 80, 101
Technical education: relationship to liberal education, 122
Technicians, narrow education of, 124

Technology, 13, 123
Text, interpretation of, 106
Textbooks, 29, 87–89
Theists, humanism of, 13–15
Theology, 4, 16, 23–24
Third Amendment, 166 n.43
Third world (Underdeveloped countries), 139–42
Thirteenth Amendment, 55, 60
Thompson, Dorothy, 139
Title I programs, 103–4
Toleration: of ambiguity of knowledge, 128–37; of conflicting beliefs, 121
Torcaso v. Watkins, 159 n.22, 169 n.84
Tracy, David, 135
Transcendence of God, 20
Truth, 31, 130–33, 134

Unbelief, protection of, 77–79, 87
Uncertainty Principle, 134
Underdeveloped countries (Third world), 139–42
Utilitarianism, 17, 56, 125–26

Validity, 134–35
Value neutrality as threat, 119, 123–24, 137, 144–48
Values, 24–25, 135, 147, 152–53; in Judaeo-Christian tradition, 28, 34, 82; needed in liberal education, 119, 123–24, 137, 144–48; religious and legal, 20–21, 32; shift from community to individualistic, 144–48
Vatican, post-liberalism in, 16
Vested interests, 152, 153
Virginia, 42–43, 114
Virtue, 42, 43, 120, 128
Vocational training, college emphasis on, 125–26, 127
Voltaire, 163 n.10
Voluntarism, religious, 12–13, 18, 52, 84–85, 115

"Wall of separation" (Jeffersonian metaphor), 41, 65, 66
Walz case, 100–101, 170 n.109
Walzser, Michael, 58, 106
Wealth, 145, 147; maldistribution of, 141, 153
Welfare mentality, 143
Welfare state, 73, 112
White, Byron, 38, 115–16, 161–62 n.1
Whitehead, Alfred North, 7, 122, 144
Williams, Roger, 42

Women, 18, 143; rights of, 23, 30, 110, 111
Woodward, C. Vann, 109–10
Working poor, 143
World affairs, deficiency in student knowledge of, 126

Yankelovitch, Daniel, 148

Zorach case, 99, 170 n. 109

ABOUT THE AUTHOR

CHRISTOPHER F. MOONEY, S.J., a member of the Pennsylvania Bar, is Professor of Religious Studies at Fairfield University. He previously served as Chair of the Theology Department at Fordham University, President of Woodstock College, Assistant Dean at the University of Pennsylvania Law School and Academic Vice President at Fairfield. He holds doctorates in both theology and law, and in recent years has had as his major interest the interface between religious and legal values. He has written six other books: *Teilhard de Chardin and the Mystery of Christ* (1966), which won the National Catholic Book Award, *The Making of Man* (1971), *Man Without Tears* (1975), *Religion and the American Dream* (1977), *Inequality and the American Conscience* (1982), and *Public Virtue: Law and the Social Character of Religion* (1986), which won the Alpha Sigma Nu Award in the Humanities.